The Findhorn Book of Community Living

by

William Metcalf

First published by Findhorn Press 2004

ISBN 1 84409 032 9

British Library Cataloguing-in-Publication Data.
A catalogue record for this book is available from the British Library.

Edited by Shari Mueller
Cover by Thierry Bogliolo
Internal design by Karin Bogliolo
Cover background photograph by Digital Vision
Cover central photograph ©PhotoDisc

Printed and bound by WS Bookwell, Finland

Published by

Findhorn Press

305a The Park, Findhorn
Forres IV36 3TE
Scotland, UK
tel 01309 690582
fax 01309 690036
e-mail: info@findhornpress.com

www.findhornpress.com

CONTENTS

ACKNOWLEDGMENTS

I want to thank the following people for checking the information which I include in this book about their intentional communities: Jan Bulman, of Windsong Cohousing, Canada; Sonia Christophe, of Lothlorien, Brazil; Richard Coates, of Findhorn Foundation, Scotland; Enid & Ian Conochie, of The Wolery, Australia; Christa Falkenstein, of ZEGG, Germany; Garry Favel and Ruth Lacey, of Kibbutz Kadarim, Israel; Monika Flörchinger, of Kommune Niederkaufungen, Germany; Justin Peters, of Darvell Bruderhof, England; Valerie Renwick-Porter, of Twin Oaks, USA; Kaz Takahashi, of Community Alternatives, Canada; and Lepre Viola, of Damanhur, Italy.

Karen Christensen and George Woodward, of Berkshire Press, USA, provided access to materials from the Encyclopedia of Community: From the Village to the Virtual World, even before it was published. Diana Leafe Christian, my Editor at Communities magazine, helped me to ensure clear and accurate writing.

When requested, vital information and sound advice was provided by Beatrice Briggs, Lucilla Borio, Sven Borstelmann, Chris Coates, David Colyer, Don Durnbaugh, Peter Forster, Insa Freese, Daniel Gavron, Robert Gilman, Daniel Greenberg, Malcolm Hollick, Linda Joseph, Julia Kommerell, Gabriela Krauskopf, Peter Lloyd, Graham Meltzer, Tim Miller, Bindu Mohanty, Michael Murray, Henry Near, Val Oliver, Yaacov Oved, Don Pitzer, Chris Sanderson, Laird Schaub, Ruth Sobol, Max Stanton, Bill Sullivan, Gina Walker and David Welch.

I want to thank Griffith University's Australian School of Environmental Studies and its Head, Dr Pat Dale, for financial, computing and research support, and Griffith University's library staff, particularly Phillip McDonald, Sharon Klein and Catherine Ashley, for helping me to locate obscure information and verify numerous details.

Karin and Thierry Bogliolo, Carol Shaw and Shari Mueller, of Findhorn Press, were supportive, friendly and professional as my publishers. If all publishers were as good as Findhorn Press, the lives of authors such as myself would be far easier.

I thank my friends Daryll Bellingham, Helen Best, Isabell Blömer, Dianne Burgess, Celia Genn, Michelle Riedlinger and Bill Smale who encouraged and supported me in various ways.

Chapter 1

UNIVERSAL DRIVE TO COMMUNITY LIVING

Perhaps Homo sapiens (wise people) should be called Homo communitas (community people), since community of one sort or another is something into which we are born, in which we live, and where we shall all die and be long remembered—or soon forgotten.

Within a strong community, particularly the small, cohesive intentional communities covered by this book, people are able to blossom and bloom. They are also more likely to feel that they have a worthwhile social niche, feel valued by others, and will almost certainly feel more secure than when living in isolation or even within a conventional nuclear family.

We humans are social, pack or herd animals, like dogs and most other mammals but not, for example, cats. We are 'hard-wired' with intense social needs to have a place within community, to belong to a group. To deprive a person of social interaction, to keep that person isolated from community, is a severe punishment. Long-term prisoners report that the worst, most-feared part of incarceration is solitary confinement.

Religiously-based groups such as the Hutterites and Amish use the threat of being shunned by other members of their intentional community as an effective motivation to change behaviour. Almost universally, parents use similar techniques to elicit acceptable behaviour by children, when they punish a child by sending him/her early to bed (physical isolation) or threaten to withhold their love (emotional isolation). For all of us, peer pressure can be a powerful determinant of how we act, try to appear, and even think—simply because we all fear the loss of community. We dread the thought of social isolation, recognising how adversely it would impact on our physical, emotional and spiritual well-being.

There have been numerous studies of the adverse impacts of solitary living on our physical and emotional health, and while the specifics differ, all agree that living alone for an extended period is associated with poorer health and a shorter lifespan. Research also suggests that while it is better to live with a partner than alone, it is better yet to live within a group or network of people with whom one can interact closely and whom one trusts—that is, within a community.

Numerous social commentators blame high levels of various social ills on the loneliness and anonymity which results from people living alone, without any sense of belonging. This is known as *anomie*, a serious social and psychological condition. Some anomic people strive for community through joining internet-based virtual communities, through anonymous interactions in bars, and through a fantasy life played out with soap operas, pornography and substance abuse.

Of course there are exceptions to this, as to all generalisations. For example, some people choose to live alone for a portion of their lives, because of the intensity of their work. Their sense of community may be achieved through colleagues. Many seekers of spiritual enlightenment choose isolation for a time, and live as a recluse, praying and/or meditating. Retreat can be a wonderful experience and is richly praised by practitioners—but it is important to note that these people have chosen social isolation rather than had it forced upon them. But even here, people in spiritual retreat are part of a spiritual community of fellow devotees, who support them with food and such. A hermit, after all, is part of the Community of Eremites.

Anthropological evidence indicates that it is at the core of our humanness to think of the world as being composed of 'us' and 'them'. Within the first group, we feel a sense of community, of interdependence and mutual responsibility, while towards the others we are suspicious and, at times, fearful.

That is why all human societies maintain boundaries. Military propagandists understand and rely on this all too human tendency when whipping up fear and detestation of the other—and convincing us that the other is so different from 'us' that it will be okay even to kill and maim 'them'.

There is a long tradition of people dropping out of their conventional communities and trying to create intentional communities, as is discussed in Chapter Three. This process, while pre-dating the industrial revolution, increased dramatically with the anomic work and social life of the machine age. The past forty years have witnessed almost an epidemic of intentional community establishment across the world. Advertisers cash in on this urgent, widely felt need for greater community by marketing new housing as a community rather than merely a suburban subdivision. My local newspaper recently ran an article in its Real Estate section saying,

> *COMMUNITY, community, community will be the next real estate catchcry as the baby boomer generation looks for "village" locations with a strong connection between residents. ... the boomers are looking for a sense of belonging and want to revert to the smaller, village-style living with good facilities, shops and cafés either within the city or nearby. (Courier Mail, 28 May 2003, p. 5)*

We humans are indeed hard-wired toward living in community, and many of us try to realise that urge through developing and/or joining intentional communities. Humans have clearly demonstrated this urgent need to be part of a community throughout recorded history—and most likely for long before then. That is why we humans should be known as Homo communitas.

∞∞∞

Community is such a broad, sweeping term that it can mean almost anything, or next to nothing. Whenever we use the term community, we need to ensure that the people with whom we communicate have the same meaning in mind.

During thirty years of participation, research and writing in this field, many people have contacted me, saying they want to live in a community (always meaning an intentional community or communal group) yet, when questioned further, what they really seem to be after is often not much more than to be able to live as an individual, or nuclear family, in a nice neighbourhood. They say they want to live in community without recognising that they are already there! As often as not, their attachment to privacy and individualism precludes a fuller experience of community even though that is what they say, and believe, that they truly want.

This book is about 'intentional community', meaning communities which people consciously create for themselves rather than those which arise naturally merely through humans living or working in close proximity.

Although I am a scholar, this book is not a scholarly treatise, but is aimed at ordinary people who wish to learn more about how others have managed to live in a more intense and supporting intentional community—and how they can move in that direction by joining or forming an intentional community. For that reason, I provide few references, although this is compensated for by the extensive list of resources at the end of this book. I tried to make this list as broad as possible, ranging from magazines and newsletters to scholarly books and journals, and have included all the community directories I can find, and a wide range of web sites. Because web sites have a habit of being changed, I can only promise that they were all active at the time of writing.

I try to be fair and objective, although I am anything but dispassionate about this topic. I do care about community in all its forms, and my 58 years of living within a wide range of communities and, more importantly, my 30 years of dedication to the rigorous study of intentional community have taught me a great deal. I am passionate about the subject. I have lived communally for about half my adult life and that helps temper my research findings with the reality of daily life, as well as cut through some of the utter nonsense which sometimes finds its way into some communities.

DEFINITIONS

In this book I use several terms which require definitions. Intentional communities are formed when people choose to live with or near enough to each other to carry out a shared lifestyle, within a shared culture and with a common purpose. These can be called communes, alternative lifestyle groups, sustainable communities or alternative communities. Families in cohousing communities, students in housing co-ops, meditators in ashrams, income-sharing workers in Israeli kibbutzim, countercultural revolutionaries in an urban commune, and sustainability advocates in rural ecovillages all live in intentional communities.

I formally define an intentional community as:

> *Five or more people, drawn from more than one family or kinship group, who have voluntarily come together for the purpose of ameliorating perceived social problems and inadequacies. They seek to live beyond the bounds of mainstream society by adopting a consciously devised and usually well thought-out social and cultural alternative. In the pursuit of their goals, they share significant aspects of their lives together. Participants are characterised by a "we-consciousness", seeing themselves as a continuing group, separate from and in many ways better than the society from which they have emerged.*

The Fellowship for Intentional Community describes an intentional community as:

> *A group of people who have chosen to work together in pursuit of a common ideal or vision. Most, though not all, share land or housing. Intentional communities come in all shapes and sizes, and display amazing diversity in their common values, which may be social, economic, spiritual, political, and/or ecological. Some are rural, some urban. Some house members in a single residence, some in separate households. Some communities raise children; some don't. Some are secular, some are spiritually based, and others are both.*

Intentional community is, of course, not just about sharing money, land or housing, but is also about the reason for sharing, i.e. the intention of members. Their easily observable social interactions, buildings, mixture of public and private spaces, and their public, collective face, are manifestations of the ideology, spirit and culture of participants. These deeper, often subconscious, elements are what make intentional communities thrive—and their absence generally leads to failure. The intention, or reason, for living in community is paramount.

Although tribal or indigenous groups generally live communally, I do not consider them to be intentional communities because they live according to their society's norms and have no intention to do otherwise. Prisoners, even though their lifestyle is communal, do not live in intentional community because they made no conscious decision or 'intention' to adopt that lifestyle. Similarly, large extended families occasionally manifest social and cultural elements which appear very similar to those found within intentional community—but they are not one simply because we do not choose our family even though we choose how to interact within that biologically determined collectivity. So, while it may be important to study and understand the 'communal' interactions within indigenous, incarcerated and familial groups, they fall outside the sphere of this book.

Cohousing, a term which was first used by McCamant and Durrett in 1988, is an increasingly popular form of intentional community. The authors say cohousing has five characteristics: participatory process, intentional neighbourhood design, extensive common facilities, complete resident management, non-hierarchal structure and separate income sources. Typically, cohousing groups have 20-40 private households, as well as a common building with a large dining room where members eat together several times per week, plus work and social space. Members commonly share equipment ranging from washing machines and power tools to computers and office equipment. Cohousing started in the 1970s in Denmark, known as 'bo*f*ælleskaber', as well as in Sweden, known as 'kollektivhuser' and the Netherlands, known as 'centraal wonen'. Cohousing groups are often in or near cities, and are oriented so that members can maintain urban employment and outside social contacts while enjoying the benefits of shared facilities and an enhanced social life although maintaining privacy and independence through having separate living spaces.

Ecovillage is, in my opinion, an overused although very useful term which refers to an intentional community where environmental sustainability is sought, along with social justice, equality, peace, etc. Some intentional communities, of course, from time immemorial have had these goals and have been more or less successful in their realisation. 'Ecovillage' was coined and popularised by Robert and Diane Gilman in their 1991 book, *Eco-villages and Sustainable Communities.* The Gaia Trust, Denmark, took up this concept and provided funding to promote ecovillages across the globe. At meetings hosted by Gaia Trust in 1993 and 1994, the idea of a Global Ecovillage Network (GEN) was developed. The first GEN meeting was held at Findhorn Foundation, Scotland, in October 1995, and the Global Ecovillage Movement was formally launched. GEN is now one of the most important communication and motivation organisations for intentional communities around the globe.

Communal, as an adjective, is important in helping to understand intentional community. While almost all humans are in some form of community, some are far more, and others far less, communal. For instance, the community of neighbours on my street is far less communal than is the large household in which I live, Mabel's Treat, although we neighbours are far more communal than is my city, Brisbane. Similarly a friendly neighbourhood is more communal than is the community within a large city apartment complex where people not only do not know each other, but have no desire to do so, yet is less communal than a cohousing group or ecovillage—and both of which are less communal than is a commune.

Commune refers to an intentional community in which most property is owned collectively, where members work together within a largely collectivised economy, and where a significant amount of social life focuses on the group which appears to members and outsiders to be a pseudo-family. The term commune is often misused by the popular media to disparage any intentional community—the implication being of dope-smoking, new-age hippies with only a modest grasp of reality.

STRUCTURE OF THIS BOOK

Findhorn Press wants this book to be a non-academic, personalised account of intentional communities around the globe. For that reason, in Chapter Two I describe myself and my involvement with this social movement. This should help readers appreciate the life experience from where I am coming, and my approach to intentional community. Should a reader feel that she/he detects some bias, in spite of my best efforts, then perhaps this will also be explained. But, while I try to be objective and fair in my writing, at times my personality and feelings show. Intentional community is a subject about which one cannot easily remain dispassionate.

It is my experience that we can only understand anything on a superficial level unless we explore its background, formative forces and history. For that reason, in Chapter Three I provide a very brief history of intentional communities and the ideas which underpin them. This will help readers appreciate that intentional communities have a long and rich tradition from which a great deal can be learned and, hopefully, inspiration gained.

I take the reader on a whirlwind tour of contemporary intentional communities from around the globe in Chapter Four. This shows how widespread is this movement, as well as demonstrating the extraordinary diversity of groups.

Chapter Five is devoted to small case studies of eleven contemporary intentional communities. These have been selected on three criteria: to describe some wonderful intentional communities; to give geographical and ideological breadth to the movement; and, most importantly, to exemplify the general points discussed within this book, particularly in Chapter Seven. Although I wrote and am responsible for these community accounts, at least one member of each group cooperated with me to ensure the accuracy of facts and the fairness of my comments.

I assume that many people who read this book will be interested in not only learning about intentional community but also in taking part, so Chapter Six specifically looks at how to join or form a group.

In Chapter Seven, I explore various social, legal, financial and political issues which are commonly found within intentional communities, and offer my observations, analysis and opinions.

One problem which plagues the intentional community movement almost everywhere in the world is the accusation that some are 'wicked cults', and the ill-informed assumption that most intentional communities have that tendency. Most books about intentional community, including my earlier works, ignore or trivialise this issue. Given the audience for whom this book is aimed, in Chapter Eight I approach the problem head-on, trying to both explain the confusion and suggest ways of coping.

I wrap up this book in Chapter Nine by looking at the future of the intentional community movement.

Finally, I provide an extensive Appendix, listing books and journals dealing with intentional communities, and list discussion groups, directories, etc. These will help readers delve into any aspect covered in this book, and provide convenient ways to contact other interested people.

And now, to introduce myself . . .

Chapter 2

MY PERSONAL INTENTIONAL COMMUNITY STORY

I was born just before the end of World War Two, on a dairy farm near Colborne, on the north shore of Lake Ontario, Canada. This farm had been in my mother's family since the 1860s, and I seemed to be related to half the people nearby. While my mother would often try to explain how I was related to this or that person, more interestingly, my memory is of having almost as close connections to those long-term neighbours who were not kin. I did not realise or appreciate it then, but I had been born into a traditional, conservative, introspective farming community—which would soon end.

Such traditional rural communities often sound rustically romantic, and frequently evoke nostalgia for a simpler, more secure past. Indeed, some of my fondest early memories are of annual farm working bees, to thresh oats, or harvest maize to fill silos with cattle-feed for the winter. At such times, half a dozen farmers would converge on each others' farms for several days, bringing horses or tractors, to accomplish tasks that would be impossible on their own. When finished on one farm, everyone would move to the next farm. No money changed hands, and the work was completed efficiently, with memorable social interactions. Watching horses and tractors, with wagons and other equipment, plus their owners, working together is a wonderful sight.

While the outside work was almost always done by men, several women (often with their children) would arrive at each farm to help prepare the huge noon meal. After the men were fed and had returned to work, we children and our mothers ate. I remember the first time I was old enough (about 8) to be allowed to work in the field, driving teams of horses as the oat sheaves were loaded—and I therefore got to eat with the men. That day, I experienced my first communal working bee and have never forgotten that powerful sense of being part of a greater community.

While these working bees were organised ahead of time, others happened spontaneously in the case of tragedy. Neighbours would help out in case of fire, severe snow storm, illness or death. Some of these farmers did not like each other, yet they worked together amicably because they were part of a strong community.

I also remember that while our farm was three kilometres (two miles) from the one room school to and from which I walked, if we children were tired or cold—or just felt like company—we could walk into most of the houses along the way and be assured of a warm fire, milk & cookies, etc. I had no fear of strangers simply because there were almost no strangers! This is a sense of security which few young people today, particularly in urban areas, will ever experience.

While my nostalgic memories might make this traditional rural community sound like a bucolic utopia, I have equally strong memories of the shadow side. Gossip was relentless and everyone seemed to know everyone else's business—in almost every detail. Should one's behaviour falter in any way, just through normal human frailty, that person would be ridiculed and censured. There was little room for innovative and creative thinking, alternative dress or unconventional relationships. Gender roles were prescribed, and sexism, racism and ageism were deeply ingrained. While I was unaware, or only vaguely aware of this during my primary school days, by my teen years I felt oppressed, and strove to escape from this smothering, overwhelming sense of community. I escaped to university.

Because most of my young contemporaries, for probably much the same reasons, also left that traditional farming community it, like so many others, has long since collapsed. Thousands of traditional communities have disappeared from western societies because people opted for individualism, just as I did.

At University of Guelph my individualism was given greater sway where, for four years, I indulged in a moderately hedonistic student community. After graduation, I worked for a large corporation which emphasised social connections within their corporate structure. We had a wonderful sense of being part of a team, which our managers promoted. That was another sort of community. I left that corporation to become a hippie, bumming around North and Central America, and Europe, staying and working wherever the spirit moved me. I thought I was part of the Age of Aquarius, although I was very vague about what that might entail beyond smoking dope, plenty of sex and having a good time without accepting responsibility.

In 1970, my partner and I travelled the famous hippie trail across Europe and Asia to Australia. This involved four months of hitch-hiking across parts of the world that are now inaccessible or at least very dangerous. We were part of what we called a 'community of travellers', all bent on new experiences and all going somewhere—albeit aimlessly. Reaching Australia with $8.00 left between us, we experienced being migrants without community. Quickly, as migrants generally do, we established networks and created our own community consisting mainly of other recent migrants plus various social misfits and outcasts.

In 1972, several of us formed an urban commune here in Brisbane, and I had my first taste of intentional community. With no idea of what might and might not work, we struggled with all sorts of problems—and had some great times—for about a year. We had a five-year-old child in this commune and I remember that she enjoyed this experience even more than did the rest of us. It was at this time when I, a postgraduate student at University of Queensland, began my serious study of intentional communities, at first simply as a means to help me understand what was happening within my own communal life.

Between 1975 and 1978, I lived and worked in Papua New Guinea, and experienced traditional, kin-based communities. As an outsider, I was often jealous of their sense of belonging and mutual aid—yet at the same time I was appalled by the levels of violence which were tolerated, and the lack of individualism. It was common for our female students to suddenly disappear from college because their families had arranged a marriage without their consent.

Girls had almost no say in the matter. Payback violence was common, and more or less accepted as a fact of life—as was domestic violence. My rose-coloured image of traditional native society and community was shattered.

Back in Australia, in 1980 I joined Pleiades, a twelve member commune in inner-city Brisbane. We never locked our doors and were a sort of hippie drop-in centre. We had a complex roster for cooking and cleaning but the inherent pseudo-anarchy (also known as puerile selfishness) of some members meant that while some of us gave and took—others just took.

As a lecturer at Griffith University, I started my Doctorate in 1980. This was a detailed study of three aspects of intentional community living: recruitment and socialisation of members, and the generation of commitment. In my doctoral field research I visited almost 100 communal groups, of all descriptions, across the globe, and read most of the scholarly books and journals in this field. I visited such famous communal groups as Findhorn Foundation, Riverside, The Farm and Twin Oaks. Findhorn Foundation became a key element of my research and my personal/spiritual life, and I have stayed there many times since, working in all sorts of departments, and am still proud to be a Findhorn Fellow.

My research insights led me to leave Pleiades commune in 1982 and, with a new partner, establish another urban commune, Mabel's Treat. For several years, six of us happily lived there—but slowly marriages, separations and employment demands broke up the group. Mabel's Treat is still my home and there are usually three or four of us living here but we are no longer a commune, although perhaps we could still be called a small intentional community.

I have researched and written seven books about historical and contemporary intentional communities, and was editor-in-charge of all intentional community materials for the four volume *Encyclopedia of Community*. As well, I am Past President of the International Communal Studies Association, and organised a major international conference on communal living, in Germany. I am also International Correspondent for *Communities* magazine.

I continue my close involvement with members of several intentional communities around the globe such as Findhorn Foundation in Scotland, ZEGG and Kommune Niederkaufungen in Germany, Damanhur in Italy,

Riverside and Heartwood in New Zealand, and Mandala, Chenrezig, Moora Moora, Cennednyss, The Wolery, Crystal Waters and Dharmananda in Australia.

I mention all this to help the reader understand who I am, and the position from which I write this book. I have personally experienced all sorts of intentional communities ranging from libertarian collectives to right-wing survivalists, from chaste, strictly religious groups to 'free-love' communes, from Swedish Steiner communities to Israeli kibbutzim. More importantly, I have integrated these personal experiences into a broad-ranging intellectual and spiritual perspective. Some of my happiest—and saddest memories are of time in intentional communities. In them I have met some of the most wonderful—and most despicable people. Intentional communities are rarely dull!

Today, when writing this book, I am 58 years old. I resigned from my tenured academic position several years ago and, although maintaining an honorary position at Griffith University, now support myself through my writing and editing, as well as casual teaching and occasional manual labour. I have been shaped by the same forces and events which underpin the intentional community movement, from the exuberance of the 1960's free-love hippie communes to the more prosaic ecovillages and cohousing groups of today.

Chapter 3

BRIEF HISTORY OF THE INTENTIONAL COMMUNITY MOVEMENT[1]

To understand and appreciate intentional community living today, we need to know at least a little about the history of the wide-ranging, popular, and both socially and environmentally significant intentional community movement. People often erroneously assume that intentional communities are a late 20th century phenomenon. On the contrary, throughout recorded history many examples can be found of people struggling to consciously create a better society—to alleviate inequality, oppression and injustice through developing intentional community.

Some Biblical scholars see prophets such as Amos, in 8th century BC, as the first recorded intentional community planner because he envisaged a social reality based on communal principles of justice and non-exploitation. Others regard this as taking too much liberty with Scriptural interpretation.

In the 4th century BC, Plato wrote *The Republic* in which he described how to develop an intentional community—a utopia. People in Plato's proposed intentional community were not to be equal, as one might have expected, but were to be ordered in social classes, and ruled by a benign dictatorship of philosopher kings. These ruling men wouldn't have private property, and would live communally sharing spouses and children. Plato argued that this was needed to develop better (genetically improved) people. A rational breeding program would ensure that these communal humans would attain

[1] see p.128.

excellence. This pseudo-science is known as Eugenics, a popular idea within 19th century communes such as Oneida, and even within a few contemporary groups. It was also popular with some 20th century social planners ranging from communist ideologues to fascists.

As far as I can determine, Homakoeion was the first intentional community which we would recognise as such today, and about which we have much information. Pythagorus developed this commune in about 525 BC in what is now southern Italy. Several hundred vegetarian communards, following mystical and intellectual paths, worked, dined and lived together, without private property, in pursuit of an ideal society. Other writers suggest that ashrams, dating from about 1500 BC, in what is now India, should have the honour of being the first intentional community, but the evidence seems to be scarce. In any event, we have a several millennia long history of intentional communities.

During the 2nd century BC, about 4000 Essenes, in what is now Israel, ate, worked and lived together in their commune overlooking the Dead Sea. Some Biblical scholars believe that Jesus Christ lived in this commune, and argue that early Christianity was shaped by his communal experiences, but other scholars dispute this.

After His death, Jesus' followers developed communes which are the forerunners of today's numerous contemporary Christian communes. Early Christian communes, based on sharing and equality, were in direct opposition to the materialistic hegemony of the Roman Empire, and were therefore countercultural. Evidence suggests that they faced many of the same issues which are faced by contemporary intentional communities.

Monasteries, which started developing in the 4th century, adopted communal living, common property, the conscious development of a 'family atmosphere', working and eating together, and rituals of prayer and song. This monastic form of intentional community is still widely followed, although it has lost popularity in the west over the past fifty years.

Several heretical and millenarian communes formed in Europe during the Middle Ages. The Cathars began in southern France and Italy during the 11th century, Waldenses began in 12th century France and, in central Europe, the Brethren of the Free Spirit arose in the 13th century and Anabaptists in the 16th century. The Diggers, a social activist group, lived in intentional community in

17th century England. They, like all the others, were violently suppressed.

The entire German city of Münster became a form of Anabaptist commune in the 1530s. People shared food, money, housing and even spouses, but they were violently suppressed by church and state, with many killed. The iron cages in which the bodies of the communal leaders were displayed still hang from the steeple of Münster's Lambertikirche, providing one of the oddest contemporary tourist sights in Germany.

The Hutterites, part of what we now call the Anabaptist tradition, formed intentional communities in many parts of Europe in the 16th and 17th century, with communal ownership, equality and a form of Christian anarchism. Anabaptist intentional communities flourish today as Hutterites in Canada, USA and Japan, and as Bruderhofs in USA, England, Germany and Australia. Because of their relatively high birth and youth retention rates, both the numbers of people involved (about 42,000) and the number of Anabaptist-based communities (almost 450) are increasing rapidly. The well-known Bruderhof, while part of the communal Anabaptist tradition, are not affiliated with the Hutterites. In spite of many setbacks and much persecution across the centuries, the various groups of Anabaptists are one of the great success stories of communal living. The well-known Amish and Mennonites are also part of this Anabaptist tradition but do not live in intentional communities as we generally understand the term, although they are still very community-minded.

Communal philosophers and practitioners during the 18th and 19th centuries, such as Étienne Cabet, Robert Owen, Charles Fourier and John Humphrey Noyes were very important in shaping the contemporary intentional community movement. They, in quite different ways, sought not to retreat to a bucolic, spiritual, non-material world, but envisioned modern intentional communities, using modern technology, to liberate people from capitalist oppression. They promoted communal living as a real option for living in a complex, industrial society.

At New Lanark, Scotland, in the early 19th century, Robert Owen demonstrated how modern technology and humane management could support creative and fulfilling social lives, overcoming environmental and health problems through communal living. Health and nutrition improved, child-care was provided, and education made available for everyone—a far cry from the lives of grinding poverty and unhealthy misery endured by most other working class people in the mill-towns of the industrial revolution. Robert Owen's semi-utopian, yet practical and prosperous experiment was publicised around the world. Several social experiments resulted from New Lanark, particularly in USA and UK, and Owen's work had a dramatic impact on town planning. New Lanark still exists but as a tourist destination rather than intentional community.

Reverend John Humphrey Noyes, in 19th century USA, saw sexual relations as being central to intentional community. He believed that monogamous marriage was a form of slavery wherein women were owned by men, and that men also suffered because such 'ownership' prevented true Christian fellowship. Noyes established Oneida commune in the mid 19th century, and instigated a form of corporate or group marriage, meaning that all adults were married to all other adult members of the opposite sex. Oneida communards were taught to expand their feelings of love and passion beyond the small, traditional family unit to include several hundred communards. They were to engage in 'horizontal fellowship' (sexual relations with other members) as a spiritual as well as a recreational act. According to Professor Klee-Hartzell, in *Communal Societies* (1996, p. 18), sexual relations at Oneida were 'the central religious sacrament of the community'. Sex was not just for procreation but more importantly for fellowship. They did not have 'free love' as some critics claimed, because relationships were controlled by the elders. All Oneida children were reared by the group, with all adults supposed to play parental roles, although some members had child care as their specific work—just as others worked in their factory or kitchen. Oneida commune thrived for over 40 years, and continues today as a prosperous corporation making fine cutlery. The original commune house is open for visitors who may stay there, particularly if they are interested in the history of this astonishing intentional community.

Many well known intentional communities started in Germany in the 17th, 18th and 19th centuries but were persecuted and forced to flee. Many of them moved to England, Australia and South America, and particularly to North America, where they flourished. Many of these were connected to Pietism and Moravianism.

The intentional community movement peaked during the mid to

late 19th century, particularly in America, Australia and England. North American intentional communities such as New Harmony, The Shakers, Amana, the Rappites, Oneida, Brook Farm and Icaria were all well known. Media interest helped disseminate the utopian theory of 'perfectibility'—that a new, ideal social reality was achievable here and now, on earth rather than in heaven. Society, they believed, was neither an organic, natural 'thing', nor resulted from God's will. Instead, society was seen as negotiable, the result of the interplay of political, social and ideological forces. To argue that people could create their own intentional community was a revolutionary concept! Most intentional communities from this era had European roots although prospering in the 'New World'.

These intentional communities were often described at length by newspapers around the globe, thereby promoting the idea that people could create their own social reality. For example, from my research with mid to late 19th century Australian newspapers, I have often seen articles about American intentional communities such as Oneida and Amana, and these ideas were then applied in the remote rural antipodes. Around the globe, local customs and culture saw communal ideology mixing with socialism, agrarian populism and various kinds of anarchism, often with radical Christian, mystical, spiritualist, anarchist and libertarian flavours—but always at the base was the idea that an ideal society was possible to achieve here on earth, now.

The first American intentional community was probably Swanendael, which was established in Delaware in 1663 by a group of Mennonites (part of the Anabaptist tradition). Swanendael, with 41 communards, was led by Pieter Plockhoy but only lasted a year. Foster Stockwell, in the *Encyclopedia of American Communes,* 1663-1963, describes 516 separate American intentional communities during 300 years since the founding of Swanendael. There have been many more than that since, of course, and today USA has a large and diverse selection of thriving intentional communities.

Canada also has a long history of intentional communities. Between 1843 and 1855, members of the Community of True Inspiration (founded in 1714 by Eberhard Gruber and Johann Rock) built Canada Ebenezer and Kenneberg communities near Niagara Falls, Ontario, but neither lasted long. Prior to the American Civil War, several freed-slave (manumitted) communities were established in British Columbia and Ontario. William Duncan established Metlakatla community in 1862 in northern British Columbia, then moved it to Alaska in 1887. British Columbia was the site for several Scandinavian intentional communities such as Bella Coola Colony (1894) and Scandia/Quatsino (1895), both Norwegian; Danevike (1897), Danish; and Sointula (1901) and Sammon Takojat (1905) both Finnish. In 1899, about 7500 Doukhobors came from Russia and established intentional communities in Saskatchewan. Between 1908 and 1912 most of these Doukhobors moved to British Columbia where many remain. Many Doukhobors originally lived in large communal houses, with little private property, much like the Hutterites of today. During World War One, many Hutterite colonies moved to western Canada to escape the military draft in USA. In 1927, Edward Wilson, styling himself Brother XII, established the Aquarian Community in British Columbia. The Emissaries established a commune in British Columbia in 1948, with well over 100 members. This has recently ceased to be an intentional community, although the Emissaries thrive at Sunrise Ranch, Colorado. Like most Canadians, when growing up I had no idea of this rich communal tradition.

England, Scotland, Wales and Ireland have a history of intentional communities ranging from socialist and artist colonies to back-to-the-land and religious communes. After 1740, Protestant refugees from Europe, known as Moravians, established Fulneck, Ockbrook and Fairfield in England, and Gracehill in Ireland. The Diggers, or True Levellers, began in 1649 as what we would now call Christian socialists, believing that all property should be shared. Their leader was Gerard Winstanley whose image has become rather distorted by many leftists. According to Chris Coates in the *Encyclopedia of Community* (p. 755), when studied, Winstanley 'seems more like the leader of a fundamentalist Christian cult than the protosocialist envisioned by Marxist historians'. Nevertheless, 'The Diggers' live today within the title of the directory of intentional communities, *Diggers and Dreamers.* The work of Robert Owen, of New Lanark, led to other intentional communities such Orbiston (Scotland), Blackwood (Wales), the Spa Field Congregationalists, Harmony Hall, and Manea Fen (England) and Ralahine (Ireland).

Some other historical UK intentional communities which fascinate me are Abode of Love (1846-1956), established in Spaxton, Somerset, by Henry

Prince, and the Children of God commune (also known as Shakers) which was established by Mary Ann Girling in London in 1870, and continued in Hampshire until her death in 1886. The most readable account of this latter commune is Pamela Pope's historical novel, *Neither Angels Nor Demons*. The best extensive coverage of UK's long experiment in intentional community is Chris Coates' well-researched and well-written book, *Utopia Britannica*.

As mentioned, Europe, particularly Germany and France, was the home of many contemporary ideas about intentional communities. Almost every conceivable form of intentional community developed—and was often forced out to other parts of the world. Despotic regimes cannot abide intentional communities. Besides the Anabaptists to which I already referred, some of the best known are Herrnhut and Rhönbruderhof in Germany, Krinitza in Russia, and Famillistere and Cómde-sur-Vestgne Phalanx in France. A number of Swedes and Finns left home to establish utopian communes, particularly in Canada, USA and Australia. Most European countries have fascinating intentional community histories, too complex to be described here.

I have discovered almost 150 intentional communities in Australia prior to 1970, and I keep finding more. Australia's first intentional community was Herrnhut, established in Victoria in 1852 by Johann Frederick Krumnow, a charismatic German. Herrnhut was named after the Moravian-Pietist commune which Count Zinzendorf, of Saxony, had established in 1727. Herrnhut prospered for some years, with about 60 members at its peak, but finally collapsed in 1889 after 37 years. Maria Heller, a German mystic, founded Australia's second intentional community, Hill Plain, in 1875, but it only lasted about a year. During the 1890s, Australia's colonial governments helped found and support almost 100 intentional communities in South Australia, Queensland, New South Wales, Tasmania and Victoria. These governments saw rural communes as an innovative way to settle people on the land and disperse troublesome urban unemployed. Australia during the 1890s probably had a higher proportion of its population living communally than would have been found anywhere else in the world. Most of these subsidised intentional communities collapsed within five years, sometimes of their own accord and sometimes because of political connivance. Since Herrnhut began in 1852, Australia has never been without at least one intentional community.

New Zealand' history of intentional communities starts with Root's Assembly, a Brethren group established by Joseph Roots in 1874 at Fielding, near Wanganui. They had their own school and church, and lived closely together, holding everything in common. They supported themselves through farming and operating a steam-powered sawmill and door factory. In 1898, Professor Alexander Bickerton formed Federative Home, an urban commune of about 30 members in Christchurch. Bickerton was interested in anarchism, socialism and eugenics, and was opposed to marriage as commonly understood. Until it closed in 1903, about 30 members lived comfortable, communal lives with their own theatre, large dining room, gymnasium, tennis court, library, etc. The next major New Zealand intentional communities comprised pacifists: Beeville, a farming group of about 30 people, established in 1933 and lasting until the mid 1970s; Tozer Community, established in 1942 with about 10 members and closing in 1945; New Life Colony, established in 1943 at Kerikeri with perhaps 5 members and closing within a year; and Riverside, established in 1941, and growing to over 70 members on a large, prosperous farm. Riverside continues today with about 30 members, making it New Zealand's oldest intentional community.

Japan also has a long tradition of intentional communities, originally based primarily on Buddhism. Some of Japan's more secular intentional communities included: Ittoen ('Garden of the One Light') which was founded by Nishida Tenko, in 1911 in Kyoto; Atarashiki Mura ('New Village') founded by Mushakoji Saneatsuin, in 1918 in Miyazaki Prefecture; and Shinkyo Dojin ('People of the Same State of Mind'), which was founded by Ozaki Masutaro, in 1939, in Nara Prefecture. All three intentional communities continue, although greatly changed. After World War Two, numerous secular and political communes were established, many having Communist connections. Few have survived although other forms of intentional community are doing well. An excellent article about Japan is by Dr Christophe Brumann in the *Encyclopedia of Community*.

Many Latin American countries have rich histories of intentional communities. The first that I know about were Christian Socialist communes, known as 'Reducciones', which the Jesuits established for the Guaraní Indians of what is now Argentina, Brazil, Paraguay and Uruguay. In 1609, the first of these intentional communities was established, and by the early 18th century, 30 communities, with perhaps 20,000 members, operated. Members worked on communally owned land, sharing production. As well as farming, they made musical instruments, artworks and even watches. Education was important and while the Jesuits maintained overall control, the Guaraní had considerable autonomy. In 1767, the Portuguese expelled the Jesuits, all Reducciones were disbanded, and the Guaraní violently dispersed. In mid to late 19th century, Welsh people established Chubut, an intentional community in Argentina, while in Paraguay numerous groups were established: The Lincolnshire Farmers, from England; San Bernardino and Nueva Germania, from Germany; Nueva Italia, from Italy; Colonia Elisa, from Sweden; Nueva Australia and Cosmé, from Australia; and New Wales, from UK. All were motivated by socialism and sometimes anarchism and mysticism. Most lasted only a few years although descendants remain there today. During the 1920s, many Mennonites (Anabaptists) established intentional communities in Belize, Bolivia, Guatemala, Mexico, Paraguay and Uruguay, and today there are 53 Old Order Mennonite colonies. In 1940-41, having been persecuted in Germany and then UK, three Hutterian Brethren colonies were established in Paraguay. Due to internal dissent and fear of government interference, however, all these colonies closed in the early 1960s with members moving to USA where they are known as Bruderhof.

While Kibbutzim are certainly the best known of Israeli intentional communities, many communal groups preceded them, such as the already mentioned Essenes (2nd and 3rd century BC). Communal monasteries have been in Palestine since the 4th century AD. Several American groups established intentional (millenarian) communities there during the 19th century. The Jerusalem Colony, founded in 1881, was joined by a group of Swedes in the 1930s, and still exists but as a luxury hotel. Degania, the first Kibbutz, was established in Palestine in 1909-10 and thrives today as the oldest of 266 communal Kibbutzim, ranging from about 40 to almost 2,000 members. Israel has not only a fascinating communal history but an equally interesting present. An excellent coverage of this history has been written by Professor Henry Near, in *The Encyclopedia of Community.*

India has an ancient tradition of intentional communities, with Buddhist Ashrams existing for several centuries BC. Bindu Mohanty, in *The Encyclopedia of Community* (p. 724), makes the important point that 'unlike the case with intentional communities elsewhere in the world, the spiritual leader or head of the ashram rarely seeks to establish a community. Rather, the number of disciples around the leader simply grows, with the result being that eventually a community develops, centered on the homestead of the leader.' Many Indian intentional communities, with more secular aims combined with spirituality, were established throughout the country with some of the best-known being: Satyagraha, established by Mohandras (Mahatma) Gandhi, near Ahmedabad, in 1915; Christavashram, established by K. Chandy, K. Mathai and M. Job, near Kottayam, in 1934; and Anandwan, established by Baba Amte, in Maharashtra, in 1949. Many very old intentional communities can be found today in India, along with a vibrant new wave starting in the late 1960s.

As far as I can determine, the Shakers' Sabbathday Lake, established in 1794 in Maine, USA, is the oldest intentional community still operating in the world today. In the early 19th century Sabbathday Lake had 150 members but this slowly declined to about a dozen, but is now growing. My suggestion that this is the oldest intentional community is based on the exclusion of older monasteries and Ashrams because of their institutional/corporate connections rather than grass-roots base. This is a very arguable (bold/erroneous?) decision, and will be contested by other scholars.

∞∞∞

The long and complex history of intentional communities gives us reason to be optimistic about creating a better, more sustainable lifestyle. Of course most historical intentional communities no longer exist—but then the same can be said about corporations, families and even nations. Historically, the longevity of intentional communities is probably similar to that of other voluntary social institutions. Most businesses, clubs, political parties and other voluntary associations like intentional communities last only a few years although a few endure for a century or more.

History reveals that the deeply-felt drive within many cultures and epochs to create intentional community is an in-built, permanent aspect of humanity—even though most specific examples of intentional communities are more transitory. This deeply-rooted human tendency thrives and is today being realised within widely divergent intentional communities, throughout much of our contemporary world, as the next chapter demonstrates.

Chapter 4

CONTEMPORARY INTENTIONAL COMMUNITIES AROUND THE GLOBE

Intentional communities are found today in all so-called 'western' countries and in many others as well. There are several excellent directories of intentional communities which are regularly updated but they cannot keep up with this dramatically changing movement. The best three directories are: *Eurotopia: Directory of Intentional Communities and Ecovillages in Europe; Communities Directory: A Guide to Intentional Communities and Cooperative Living* (mainly covering North America); and *Diggers & Dreamers: The Guide to Communal Living* (mainly covering England, Scotland, Wales and Ireland). There are also several smaller directories, some of which are web-based, as shown in the Appendix.

In this chapter, I shall, to the best of my abilities, and given the information available and the limited space available, help readers gain an overview of the global intentional community movement. While not every country can be discussed, I include the major players, with the choice of intentional communities being based on my professional knowledge and opinions.

USA & CANADA

Communities Directory provides information on 584 North American intentional communities. Their database, however, contains information on 1,937 intentional communities, but apparently only about 30% even want their names to be published. Given that there will be other groups not even on this database, it is reasonable to assume that there are over 2,000 intentional communities in USA and Canada. All indications are that this movement is healthy and growing.

Laird Schaub, in *The Encyclopedia of Community* (p. 759), suggests several reasons why the majority of intentional communities do not appear even in a directory which has been put together with so much care and attention, by people who are all involved in that movement:

> *Some are not looking for new members; some cannot commit to responding to inquiries; some prefer to recruit through word of mouth only; some are looking for a specific kind of member and the Directory is too broad based; some are concerned about unwanted attention from people who do not agree with their values or practices; and some are not interested in connections with the Communities Movement.*

Schaub also points out that the Fellowship for Intentional Community learns about 'new groups at the rate of about one per week (that includes both start-ups and groups discovered after being in existence for years). Thus, it is a highly fluid field of information.' I fully agree with Schaub's observations because, even though I have been actively involved in intentional community research for 30 years, I frequently discover communal groups, even near where I live, about which I have not previously heard. Schaub's reasons apply just as well to the other directories mentioned in this book, as well as to scholars such as myself. Remember, this is a very dynamic social movement.

Depending on definitions, and bearing in mind the limitations applying to any attempt to provide accurate statistics about this movement, Laird Schaub estimates that 'perhaps' 100,000 North Americans (about 0.03% of the population) live in intentional communities today, 'even with the most liberal definition of the term'.

Throughout North America there are many well-known intentional communities, with some of the best known being: Alpha Farm (Oregon); Ananda (California); Community Alternatives (British Columbia); Earthhaven (North Carolina); East Wind (Missouri); Ganas (New York); Goodenough (Washington); Koinonia (Georgia); Lama (New Mexico); Padanaram (Indiana); Sirius (Massachussets); Sunrise Ranch (Colorado); The Farm (Tennessee); and Twin Oaks (Virginia). Twin Oaks and Community Alternatives are described in the next chapter.

Anabaptist intentional communities flourish as Hutterites and Bruderhofs. According to Max Stanton, a leading Hutterite researcher, in early 2003 about 40,400 Hutterites were living communally in 436 colonies in Manitoba, Alberta, Saskatchewan and British Columbia in Canada, and in North Dakota, South Dakota, Washington, Minnesota and Montana in USA. On average, each colony has about 100 adults and children although they range from 33 to 181. This is a rapidly growing segment of the intentional community movement with another 23 colonies due to open by the end of 2004. Hutterites are divided into three 'leut', meaning people, congregation or group: Dariusleut, Lehrerleut and Schmiedeleut. The differences depend more on history and cultural practices than on religious, doctrinal differences. In Hutterite colonies, all property is owned in common and most members work together on their large, collective farms, using modern farm technology, and live together in large communal buildings.

About 2,000 people live in seven Bruderhof communities in USA: New Meadow Run and Spring Valley, in Pennsylvania; and Woodcrest, Catskill, Fox Hill, Bellvale and Maple Ridge, in New York state. Unlike the farm-based economy of the Hutterites, Bruderhofs earn income from businesses, the most important being Community Playthings, which produces wooden toys and classroom furniture, high quality items which sell to the general public as well as to public schools and child welfare programs. The Bruderhof also established a business called Rifton Equipment for People with Disabilities, which makes a wide range of therapeutic and recreational items for the 'physically challenged', particularly children. The Bruderhof's Plough Publishing House publishes and sells a wide range of material on social justice, pacifism and religion, although members regard this more as outreach, or witnessing, than as a money-making venture. Another Bruderhof business designs, makes and installs signs. Collectively, the Bruderhof are a prosperous and productive people.

About 30,000 Dukhobors live in close-knit communities in western Canada with a few in Oregon and California. Most have abandoned the communes in which they first lived in Canada, although some, such as New Settlement, in British Columbia, still follow the old ways to some extent. The Dukhobors have been subjected to considerable government interference over the past century because of their anti-conscription stance, pacifism, anarchism, unwillingness to own land or swear an oath, and various forms of non-violent protest. There seems to be much less of this opposition and persecution today as most Dukhobors seem to be blending into the wider society.

Many cohousing groups are springing up, and this is certainly a key part of the future of the North American intentional community movement. Three well known examples are Doyle Street (purpose-built) and N-Street (retrofitted), both in California, and Windsong (purpose-built) in British Columbia. Windsong is described in more detail in the next chapter. A few cohousing groups, such as Nyland (Colorado), are in rural areas but most are urban or suburban. Cohousing groups are generally very family and environmentally-oriented, often maintaining a liberal, sophisticated urban culture.

Numerous ecovillages are being formed, generally with clearly stated environmental aims, and often with a spiritual but non-religious flavour. Most of them belong to the large and rapidly growing Global Ecovillage Network, whose North, South and Central American headquarters are at The Farm, a large, 32-year-old intentional community in Tennessee. Dancing Rabbit (Missouri), Earthhaven (North Carolina) and Los Angeles Eco-Village (California) are some of the best-known examples.

Religiously-oriented intentional communities also appear frequently, although most adamantly wish **not** to be associated with the term intentional community. New examples of what we think of as 1960's style hippie communes still occasionally form, as do examples of other, more extreme forms such as survivalist communes. While some North American intentional communities challenge sexual and social norms through group marriages, strange dietary habits, unusual rituals, etc., and some are on the political fringe, most are content to do their own thing without being particularly countercultural.

The North American intentional community movement is healthy, with many well-established communities, several over a century old, and a range of new groups being formed. North America is also the home of several important support facilities for this movement, including The Fellowship for Intentional Community, publisher of *Communities Directory* and *Communities* magazine, and the Communal Studies Association, publisher of the academic journal *Communal Societies*. One of the two most important academic centres in the world for the study of intentional communities, The Center for Communal Studies, is at University of Southern Indiana (the other is Department of Communal Research, Yad Tabenkin Research and Documentation Center of the Kibbutz Movement, in Israel).

LATIN AMERICA

Throughout Latin America, intentional communities have developed, particularly over the past decade. There is no satisfactory directory of these intentional communities although some can be found in other directories and on various web sites. Some of the best-known intentional communities in this part of the world are Huehuecoyotl, Krutsio and Los Horcones, in Mexico; Atlantis, in Columbia; Waldos, in Ecuador; Komunidad Janajpacha, in Bolivia; and Communidade De Londrina and Lothlorien, in Brazil. Lothlorien is described in the next chapter. Some, such as La Senda and La Hermita, both in Mexico, call themselves ecovillages. According to Gering in *The Encyclopedia of Community*, about 75,000 Mennonites, having left Russia in the late 19th century, now live in 53 colonies in Latin America. More can be learned about intentional communities in Latin America in my article in *The Encyclopedia of Community.*

ENGLAND, SCOTLAND, WALES AND IRELAND

Diggers & Dreamers: The Guide to Communal Living, compiled by a dedicated group of intentional community supporters, lists 84 intentional communities but they tell me they have about 400 on their database, as well as some 250 Housing Cooperatives, of which perhaps 10% have communal households. Another 109 lay and 31 religious orders appear in another listing, leading Chris Coates, one of the editors, to estimate that there are about 500 intentional communities now operating in UK. For the same reasons as previously quoted from Laird Schaub, many UK intentional communities simply do not appear in directories.

Peter Lloyd's *Spiritual Britain: A Practical Guide to Today's Spiritual Communities, Centres & Sacred Places,* takes a slightly different look at the intentional community movement. Lloyd lists 64 groups (not all are intentional communities). His long association with Findhorn Foundation obviously shaped his selection process for this informative and useful book.

In *The Encyclopedia of Community* (p. 757), Chris Coates estimates that about 10,000 people are living in intentional communities in the UK today, suggesting an average community size of about 20. He states that more UK people are now living in intentional communities than ever in the past, and that networks are developing for a wide range of groups, one good example being 'Radical Routes', a network of Housing Cooperatives. Coates also describes 'groups of New Age travellers moving from mobile communities to more permanent land-based settlements, low-impact living groups experimenting with sustainable lifestyles and an embryonic cohousing movement'.

In the previous chapter I discussed historical British intentional communities such as New Lanark which influenced this movement throughout the world. Today, the Findhorn Foundation, established in Scotland in 1962, has much the same international impact. It is not only the best known and largest intentional community in UK, but its obviously successful way of combining 'new age' beliefs and spiritual practices with humanism, environmental sensitivity and social innovation is a model which many intentional communities around the globe seek to emulate—although most fall far short. As will be seen in the next chapter, Findhorn Foundation is far from perfect but it is an intentional community with a significant global impact.

There are, of course, many other well-known intentional communities. Whiteway, established in 1898 in Gloucestershire, is probably the oldest intentional community still operating, although it has changed greatly from the Victorian era of its establishment. Some other well known intentional communities, and dates of establishment, are Laurieston Hall (Dumfries & Galloway, 1972), Old Hall (Essex, 1974), People in Common (Lancashire, 1974), Centre for Alternative Technology (Powys, 1975), Redfield (Buckingham, 1978), Brithdir Mawr (Pembrokeshire, 1994) and Hockerton Eco-Hamlet (Nottinghamshire, 1995).

About 500 people live in two Bruderhof colonies, Darvell (Sussex, 1971) and Beechgrove (Kent, 1995). The members are mainly American, and while trying to mix well and cooperate with their neighbours, they have little to do with other intentional communities. Much can be learned about intentional community living from the Bruderhof, but that seems more likely to happen in USA than in UK, although the reasons are unclear. Darvell Bruderhof is described in more detail in the next chapter.

Compared to North America, UK intentional communities are more likely to be urban, often to be found in old Victorian or Edwardian mansions and retrofitted housing. The Global Ecovillage Movement was formally launched at Findhorn Foundation in 1995 although, of course, many intentional communities around the globe had been following this ideology and lifestyle for ages. Cohousing seems to have come to UK from its origins in Denmark, but via USA. Complex land-use and financial regulations have so far made this form of intentional community less viable than in other parts of Europe or North America, but several groups such as Community Project at Lewes (Sussex, 1998) and Stroud Cohousing (Gloucester, 2000) are under way and, as far as I know, are doing well.

GERMANY

Germany has one of the largest and most diverse intentional community movements. *Eurotopia: The Directory of Intentional Communities and Ecovillages in Europe* lists 101 contemporary German groups, although there are many more not included. Some of the best known are Kommune Niederkaufungen, Lebensgarten Steyerberg, Lebensgut Pommritz, Öko Lea, Ufa-Fabrik and ZEGG. All of these have grown out of the countercultural and environmental movements, often mixed with anarchism, feminism and socialism. Kommune Niederkaufungen and ZEGG are described in the next chapter.

Germany has numerous religiously-based intentional communities such as Agnus Dei, Basisgemeinde Wulfshagenerhütten, and Freie Christliche Gemeinde Bethsehel (all Christian), Gemeinschaft Oberbronnen (Twelve Tribes), and Nava Jiyada Nrsimha Ksetra (Hare Krishna). Some intentional communities such as Camphill Dorfgemeinschaft Lehenhof, Stiftung Synanon, and Neubeginn have strong social work goals, helping people with psychological and social problems to recover through communal living. Although the Bruderhof started in Germany in 1920, today only one Bruderhof commune, 'Sannerz', with 15 members, exists near Fulda. There are two intentional community networks, 'Come Together' and 'Kommuja', but the movement is often divided along ideological, and occasionally personal lines.

Several intentional communities call themselves ecovillages but, as in other countries, this does not necessarily mean that they are any more environmentally sound than are other groups. Some of the best known ecovillages are Lebensgarten Steyerberg and Ökodorf Sieben Linden.

Most of the recent growth in intentional communities has occurred in the former East Germany where land is cheaper and more available than in the west. Also, in this region it is often possible to cheaply acquire large buildings which facilitate communal life. Many German intentional communities are urban communes although the trend is to move to the countryside. Most intentional communities have environmental and spiritual motivations tacked onto whatever originally motivated members.

FRANCE

For a host of political and cultural reasons, the intentional community movement is weaker here than in neighbouring Germany or Great Britain. *Eurotopia* lists 33 French intentional communities with some of the best known being Taizé and the three l'Arche communities: La Borie Noble, Saint-Antoine and Flayssière, part of a movement which has been functioning since 1948. Longo Mai, established in 1973 and now with about 80 members, is also well known. Some intentional communities have religious bases, such as Association Bouddhiste Zen-Kwan Um (Buddhist), Communauté le Surgeon (Christian) and Communauté de Sus (Twelve Tribes). The latter, with about 130 members, is probably France's largest intentional community. Bio-Lupin and Montbel Eco-Village are part of the Global Ecovillage Network, while Institut de Santé Globale, and L'Espérance have more therapeutic aims. More details can be learned from Jean-Michel Pochat's article in *The Encyclopedia of Community.*

THE NETHERLANDS

The Netherlands has a vibrant intentional community movement, with the best known being Hobbitstee (established 1969) and Humaniversity (1978). *Eurotopia* only lists 13, a small fraction of what really exists. The government and media are more supportive of intentional communities than is the case in nearby Germany, Belgium or France.

A popular form of intentional community is 'woongroepen', a communal household, usually with four to ten young members, and often located near Universities. Hundreds of these are located in most cities and towns. Members come and go but the group may last for many years. Woongroepen seem to be a hybrid of urban commune and shared student houses.

Cohousing, known as 'centraal wonen', and dating from 1977, is a very popular form of intentional community, with most groups having between 30 and 70 households. Today there are about 100 of these groups, as well as about 200 cohousing type communities for the elderly and for others who need care. Most of these receive some government support.

There are also several Christian intentional communities such as Effeta-Gemeenschap (established 1979), Franciscaans Milieuproject (1991), Het Arensnest (1981), Stichting Elim (1975) and Woongroep H.U.G.O. (1978).

BELGIUM

Compared with Germany, Netherlands and UK, Belgium has a small intentional community movement with none being well-known internationally. A popular and growing form is 'gemeenschapshuizen', i.e. small urban communes with less than ten members, often located near universities. While these typically have high membership turnover, many have lasted for a long time. Belgium also has a number of intentional communities which are like cohousing, and several, such as De Ark Gemeenschap Antwerpen, L'Arche Communauté de Bierges, and De Ark Gemeenschap Moerkerke, have a spiritual base and therapeutic/social work aims.

SCANDINAVIA

Many intentional communities are spread throughout Scandinavia although few are well known internationally other than Christiania which was established in Copenhagen, Denmark, in 1971 and now has almost 1,000 residents. The intentional community movement is popular and growing throughout

Scandinavia. *Eurotopia* lists 8 intentional communities in Denmark, 7 in Finland, 2 in Norway and 11 in Sweden but these are only a fraction of those in existence.

Cohousing is very popular, particularly in Denmark and Sweden, where it has long been encouraged by governments and is now fairly mainstream.

Ecovillages are also common throughout the area with well-known examples being Fjordvang, Ibsgaarten, Munkesøgård, Økosamfundet Dyssekilde, and Svanholm, all in Denmark; Katajamäki and Kaijanniemi, in Finland; Kilden Økosamfunn, in Norway; and EKBO, Solbyn, Understenshöjden and Tugglite, in Sweden.

Some Scandinavian intentional communities have strong religious ties such as Enonkosken Luostariyhteisö, Finland (Christian), and ISKCON: The Bhaktivedanta Book Trust, and Järna-Almviks Gård, both in Sweden (Hare Krishna). Intentional communities such as Foreningen Staffansgården and Mickelsgården in Sweden as well as Solborg in Norway, being part of the Camphill movement, have very strong social therapy goals. More information can be gained about this area by reading Jan Bang & Peter Bakker's article in *The Encyclopedia of Community*.

EASTERN EUROPE AND RUSSIA

Under Communism, intentional communities, as we use the term, were not possible simply because the official Communist Party line was that the entire society was an intentional community. Since 1990, numerous intentional communities have developed throughout this region as people try to cope with dramatic changes. Ralf Gering, in *The Encyclopedia of Community*, makes an important distinction between those intentional communities which depend on ideology imported from the west, and those which hark back to traditional, pre-communist days.

Of the foreign instigated intentional communities, Gering includes ISKCON which has started Hare Krishna centres in Bosnia-Herzegovina, Bulgaria, Croatia, Czech Republic, Estonia, Hungary, Latvia, Lithuania, Macedonia, Poland, Romania, Russia, Slovakia, Slovenia and the Ukraine. He also reports that The Fellowship of Independent Missionary Communities (formerly known as The Family of God) has intentional communities, known as 'charter homes', in Albania, Armenia, Bosnia and Herzegovina, Bulgaria,

Croatia, Czech Republic, Hungary, Kazakhstan, Latvia, Lithuania, Moldova, Poland, Romania, Russia, Slovakia, Slovenia, the Ukraine and Uzbekistan. Many intentional communities with therapeutic ends, such as the Camphill Movement, now have centres in the Czech Republic, Estonia, Poland and Russia. REMAR and RETO are two neo-Pentecostal groups with therapeutic communities in Bulgaria, Croatia, Poland and Russia. All these groups are growing rapidly.

Gering (p. 714) points out that indigenous intentional communities 'come in all colors. They can be influenced by Buddhism, Russian Orthodox Christianity, shamanism or by Western esoteric movements or communities such as Anthroposophy or Findhorn'. These intentional communities include ecovillages in Russia such as Nevo Ecoville and Rysovo Ecoville, both founded in 1992, and Ecovillage Grishino (1993), all part of the Global Ecovillage Network. Several others, such as Camphill Village Svetlana, and Kitezh Children's Ecovillage (both 1992) combine ecovillage and therapeutic aims. As an example, Gering describes (p. 715) Kitezh, with 50 residents, as being named after a legendary, invisible Utopian city and tries to address the terrible poverty that abounds in Russia. Its aim is to have fifty families and 200 children, although its progress has been very slow in recent years. Kitezh tries to emulate the closeness and warmth of ancient Russian village life. Most residents have a Russian Orthodox background and a small wooden chapel is being built in traditional Russian style. The spiritual ideal of the community is based on the life and work of the St. Sergey Radonezhsky, who, according to the community, was the first Russian Orthodox to create a monastery in the fourteenth century as a spiritual working community.

The best known intentional community today in Russia is Ecopolis Tiberkul, established in Siberia in 1992, and whose 3,000 vegan members follow the spiritual teachings of Sergej Toropa, now known as Vissarion. His theology combines New Age concepts with belief in UFOs, Christianity and Theosophy, all mixed with Russian folklore. Not surprisingly, they have been accused of being a dangerous cult and have received a bad press. I have met several members and found them to be happy and self-confident but, not having been there, cannot comment further.

Other intentional communities which are becoming better known include: Gyûrûfû Alapínyá which was founded 1991, with 31 members, and Somogyvámos which was founded in 1993, with 96 members (both in Hungary); and Dobrowka, founded in 1980, with 90 members, in Poland. Throughout eastern Europe and Russia the intentional community movement is growing both in the number of communities and membership.

ITALY

As mentioned previously, the first known intentional community was Homakoeion, established in Italy in the sixth century, BC. Although the Italian intentional community movement is small compared to that in Germany, it nevertheless thrives, with new communities developing. *Eurotopia* lists 24 intentional communities, although there are far more than this. Some of those better known are Ecovillage Upacchi, La Commune di Bagnaia, Torri Superiore and Utopiagia. Many of these intentional communities are part of the Global Ecovillage Network.

Beyond a doubt, Italy's largest and best known intentional community is Damanhur, established in 1977 in the Alpine foothills near Turin. Damanhur is really a Federation of semi-autonomous communities with a population of about 600 residents. It has its own currency, a daily paper, and perhaps 50 businesses. Damanhur is described in the next chapter.

Some intentional communities have religious affiliations such as Ananda Assisi (Yogananda), ISKCON Firenze (Hare Krishna), Commità della Guedrara (Christian), Osho Miasto (Osho), and Cooperativo di Bordo and Instituto Lama T. Kapha (Buddhist). Il Chicco has therapeutic/social welfare aims. Most intentional communities combine environmentalism and egalitarianism with their other objectives. More can be learned about Italian intentional communities in Lucilla Borio's article in *The Encyclopedia of Community.*

SPAIN AND PORTUGAL

Long considered to be a backwater of the intentional community movement, *Eurotopia* now lists 19 Spanish and 4 Portuguese intentional communities. The best known Portuguese intentional community is Tamera, founded in 1995 and a sister community of ZEGG, Germany. Tamera has about 70 members on a 134 hectare property near Monte do Cerro, and is part of the

Global Ecovillage Network. Probably the best known Spanish intentional community is Los Molinos de Rio de Aguas, established in 1986, with about a dozen members.

Several intentional communities have been created in Spain by people reclaiming abandoned peasant villages in the Pyrenean foothills. The best known are Artosilla, Aineto and Ibort where about 70 people live. Similarly, Lakabe has about 30 residents. All of these are part of Global Ecovillage Network.

As elsewhere, some Iberian intentional communities have religious affiliations such as Bio-Sol (Christian), while others are oriented towards therapy/social work, such as Argayall, and Comunidad Walden.

ISRAEL

Israel has 268 communal Kibbutzim, ranging in size from about 40 to almost 2,000 members, with a mean population of 430. At last census, 115,300 Israelis (about 2% of Israel's population) were living communally, by far the largest proportion found anywhere. This almost century-old intentional community movement is of significant, although decreasing, importance within the Israeli economic and political system. Since Kibbutz membership peaked in the mid 1980s, the number of kibbutzniks has decreased at a modest annual rate of about 0.5%. The oldest kibbutz, Degania, was established in 1909 and continues with two branches having a total population of about 830.

In 1988, I was based in Israel at the Department of Communal Research, Yad Tabenkin Research and Documentation Center of the Kibbutz Movement, one of the two great academic research centres in the world which focuses on intentional communities (the other is Center for Communal Studies, University of Southern Indiana, in USA). I conducted research at several kibbutzim, including Bet Ha Emek, Degania, Ein Harod, Gesher, Givat Brenner and Palmachim, and was impressed with their communal spirit and commitment. I was also impressed with their social security from birth to death, their economic dynamism, and kibbutznik's apparent happiness and contentment. I also observed that many kibbutzniks were involved, even in some small way, in promoting peace and goodwill with their Palestinian neighbours. When I returned in 1995, all these features appeared to have decreased.

Since the mid to late 1980s, the political and economic tide in Israel has turned against Kibbutzim, several have closed and membership is decreasing. Most are privatising facilities and functions such as schools and dining rooms—unthinkable 25 years ago. While communal child-rearing was a hallmark of kibbutz life, today nearly all kibbutz children live with their parents in traditional nuclear families. This change has been very expensive because living quarters have had to be re-designed. It has also had the effect of removing many women from the workforce, and confining them to domestic duties—a change which would have dismayed their communal grandmothers.

As Daniel Gavron, author of *The Kibbutz: Awakening from Utopia,* sadly states in *The Encyclopedia of Community* (p. 727):

> *Kibbutzim were for almost a century, an integral part of the ... Israeli nation. Seeking to lead the mainstream society, it succeeded for several decades in influencing social norms, and even to some extent in setting the national tone. When the state of Israel was established in 1948, a third of its government and twenty-six of the 120 members of its parliament were members of kibbutzim; today, none are. Ultimately Israeli society and the world at large have proved too strong. Not only has the kibbutz failed to foster universal egalitarian and communal norms, it has itself succumbed to current Western materialist and individualist values.*

Being an optimist, I admire the kibbutz movement, particularly some of the more progressive (in my eyes) kibbutzim such as Lotan, Tamuz and Tzorah. I am also impressed with members of the Green Kibbutz Movement, kibbutzniks who try to bring environmental concerns to the centre of kibbutz life. Other Israelis are modifying the traditionally rural kibbutz model to urban living, creating what we would call urban communes. I have several kibbutzniks as personal friends and share their sadness over slippage in the communal core of kibbutz life, but I am also impressed by the counter trends which I detect. Kadarim kibbutz is described in the next chapter.

INDIA

There are several hundred intentional communities in India, mostly ashrams from a wide range of religious traditions, and following diverse spiritual practices. The best guide to these is probably *From Here to Nirvana,* by

Anne Cushman and Jerry Jones, which provides information about 70 or so ashrams. Their listing is far from complete as is the case with every other directory of intentional communities.

Many intentional communities have very strong outreach or social service objectives. One good example of this is Anandwan ('Forest of Bliss') established in 1949 in Maharashtra state, for the benefit of lepers, handicapped children and homeless women. Today, about 5,000 people live in this thriving community, supporting themselves through farming and other businesses. Following Anandwan's model, four other social service oriented intentional communities started in the area. Other examples include Mitraniketan ('Abode of Friends') in Kerala, whose members promote education and appropriate development within poor rural areas, Kanavu ('Dream') in Kerala, and Namma Bhoomi ('My Land') in Karnataka. Another good intentional community of this sort, with which I have been associated for a decade, is Christavashram, in Kerala. It was established in 1934, and its members continue to provide a communal home and training facilities for orphans and others in need.

India's best-known intentional community is Auroville in Tamil Nadu state, where 1,600 people from 35 countries live. Based on the teachings of Sri Aurobindo, Auroville was founded in 1968 under the leadership of Mirra Alfassa, 'The Mother'. Auroville was envisioned as a place where people from all nationalities could live in peace and harmony. Today, it is part of the Global Ecovillage Network, with numerous educational and outreach programs.

Probably the second best-known intentional community is Osho Commune International, in Maharashtra state. This was founded in 1974 by Rajneesh Chandra Mohan, a university lecturer who became a guru known as Bhagwan Shree Rajneesh. Cushman and Jones, in *From Here to Nirvana* (pp. 215-6) describe Osho Commune International as:

> *Not your typical Indian ashram. A New Age Xanadu that attracts thousands of visitors every day, the commune is a self-contained personal growth conglomerate, offering an astonishing variety of classes and workshops in everything from organisational development to tantric sex. And, if the courses don't interest you, you can spend your days romping in the swimming pool, sauna, "Zennis" courts, and bistro of the commune's "Club Meditation".*

According to Bindu Mohanty, in *The Encyclopedia of Community* (p. 726), new intentional communities are being formed all the time with some of the more recent ones being Malamad, Good Earth Hamlet, Mitradham and Nav Darshana, all involved in ecological farming in southern India. Mohanty describes Fireflies, in Karnataka state, as 'an ashram without a guru', whose members try to live sustainable lives by following new eco-social paradigms. The intentional community movement thrives, and increasingly meets the diverse needs of India's multifaceted society.

JAPAN

Japan has hundreds of intentional communities, with most having a strong environmental ethic within either a spiritual or secular form. One of the best known is Yamagishi Kai which started in 1958 and now has about 1,600 adults, plus children, in 37 communes. One of these, Yamagishi Toyosato, with about 700 participants, is the largest intentional community in Japan. They operate a highly integrated organic farming business where the manure from 600,000 chickens is applied to 80 hectares of rice fields from which fermented rice straw is fed to 900 dairy cows. The cow and pig manure is mixed with saw dust and bark, producing compost which is applied to fields where fruit and vegetables are grown. Their sales of eggs, milk, rice, pork, fruit and vegetables results in a multi-million dollar income.

Ittoen ('Garden of the One Light') community, Kyoto, was established in 1911, and now has about 300 members who operate businesses including a construction company, printing works, commercial research institute, plus state-recognised schools and a college.

Atarashiki Mura ('New Village'), in southern Japan, was founded 1918. It nearly collapsed during the Second World War but today about 30 communards support themselves through agriculture.

In *The Encyclopedia of Community* (p. 740), Christoph Brumann pithily states, 'both Ittoen and Atarashiki Mura have opened public museums celebrating the achievements of their founders but no longer proselytize actively'. This suggests they may be in decline, perhaps going through what Professor Don Pitzer has called 'Developmental Communalism'.

Owa Hutterian Brethren is a small Hutterite colony, established in 1970 on Honshu Island, and today has about 40 members.

The best-known intentional community is Aum Shinrikyo ('Aum Supreme Truth'), founded by Asahara Shoko in about 1989. For a host of obscure reasons, they attacked the Tokyo Subway system with nerve gas in 1995, killing 12 people and injuring about 5,000. Asahara Shoko and many followers were arrested, as authorities tried to close the community. In 1997, the American government declared Aum Shinrikyo to be 'a terrorist organization'. The group continues, now known as Aleph, and is estimated to have about 500 members in 28 communities. This is a good example of an intentional community which ran off the rails, as discussed in Chapter Eight.

The 1995 nerve gas incident led to a strident, anti-cult media frenzy which adversely affected most Japanese intentional communities, particularly those of Yamagishi Kai. Although Yamagishi are non-violent pacifists, and had no connection to Aum Shinrikyo, they nevertheless were seen as a danger to society, and suffered serious consequences. The intentional community has not recovered from this anti-cult frenzy, and although new groups are forming the overall number of participants is stable or declining.

NEW ZEALAND

Barbara Knudsen's *Eco-villages & Communities in Australia and New Zealand* lists only five intentional communities, a small fraction of those currently existing. A more comprehensive listing is *Chip 'n' Away*, a newsletter which networks between intentional communities. Dave Welch, a member of Heartwood Community, frequently updates this listing, showing over 40 active intentional communities with others being formed. The main concentrations are in Coromandel Peninsula and Northland, plus the Christchurch and Nelson Districts. Most intentional communities are rural.

Riverside community was established in 1941 by anti-conscription, Christian pacifists. This amazing intentional community still thrives although it has become more secular. Their lovely church now hosts community dinners, meetings, and dances. When I first visited Riverside in the early 1980s, 70 members farmed 200 hectares with dairying and fruit production as their chief income source. When I visited Riverside for Christmas 1996, their membership had visibly decreased and aged, although their communal spirit seemed strong. When Riverside celebrated its 60th birthday in 2001, it only had 36 members. Although not without problems, Riverside is New Zealand's unrivalled intentional community success story.

Another wonderful New Zealand story of intentional community concerns Heartwood which started in Christchurch in 1971 when several social activists pooled their money to purchase a large old house for an urban commune. Members wanted to live communally while working toward creating a new society. They soon bought an adjoining house and a small farm, and established a cooperative bakery. I first visited in 1980 as part of my PhD research, then I visited again in late 2002, when I found about 25 members living in their two urban and one rural centres. Each group runs its own affairs, with its own budget, but all are linked through common ownership and an overall community budget. Any urban intentional community which manages to prosper for three decades is a rare success story.

Other well-known intentional communities include Happisam, Rainbow Valley, Renaissance and Tui, all on the South Island, plus Ahu Ahu Ohu, Bodhinyanarama, Friends Settlement, Karma Choeling Buddhist Monastery, Mahamudra and Wilderland on the North Island. Many are 25-30 years old, mature intentional communities, with stable memberships.

New Zealand's largest intentional community is Gloriavale Christian Community, with about 300 members, near Lake Haupiri on the west coast of South Island. Neville Cooper, alias Hopeful Christian, started this group in Christchurch in 1969. They moved to nearby Springbank in 1970 where the Cooperites (or Cust Community) as they were then known, sought to use modern technology to live a Christian, communal life. I stayed there in 1981 when their 40 members ran a small, intensive farm with some members working off-site and pooling all income. They lived as a full commune in a large farmhouse and adjoining buildings. They endured considerable police and media attention because of allegations of cult-like behaviour and exploitative sexual practices. In 1991, they moved to Lake Haupiri. In 1995 Neville Cooper was imprisoned for a year for 'indecent assault on community members', but he remains as their spiritual leader. Gloriavale Christian Community operates high tech businesses including maintaining helicopters and aeroplanes. They have little to do with, and are shunned by, the rest of

New Zealand's intentional community movement.

Although many intentional communities follow ecovillage principles, only some, such as Tui, near Takaka, Awaawaroa and Otamatea, near Auckland, and Valley Farm, near Paeroa, have adopted the ecovillage title and identify with the Global Ecovillage Network. Anahata Eco-village, with 23 adults, is now developing on the site of the (in)famous but now-deceased Centrepoint community, near Auckland. Silkwood Park and Otautahi ecovillages are forming.

New Zealand has a small and struggling cohousing movement. Earthsong Eco-neighbourhood, near Auckland, is the only operating group although some consider Beachcomber Community, in a former Christchurch motel, to also be cohousing. Several New Zealand groups are interested in the cohousing model of urban intentional community, so this part of the movement will probably grow.

AUSTRALIA

Australia has between 100 and 200 intentional communities, and the movement is growing. Many communities are quite small with only a few, such as Tuntable Co-operative (1973), New Govardhana (1976), Bundagen (1981), Billen Cliffs (1982), and Crystal Waters (1988) having more than 100 people. Just as in North America and UK, Australia has a wide range of religious, spiritual and secular communities, some with strong charismatic leaders while others follow consensus or democratic governance. Several communities are members of the Global Ecovillage Network, with Crystal Waters and Kookaburra Park (1993), both in Queensland, being the best known. Many intentional communities have long followed directions similar to those of the Global Ecovillage Network anyhow, and while some call themselves ecovillages, others do not accept the term.

Barbara Knudson's *Eco-villages & Communities in Australia and New Zealand*, lists only 31 intentional communities. The reasons why the majority of groups were missed have already been explained. The main area is northern New South Wales, known as the Rainbow Region, with other concentrations on Queensland's Sunshine Coast and inland from Cairns, the south west of Western Australia, and within an arc 100 kms from Melbourne, Victoria. Over time, Australian intentional communities become less radical and countercultural, individualism takes over from communalism, and they slowly blend into the larger society. This can either be seen as evidence of the failure of their communal ideals—or else their social and political maturity.

Australia's first cohousing group, Cascade Cohousing, started in 1991 in Tasmania. Cohousing Cooperative, also in Tasmania, and Pinakarri, in Western Australia, have recently started, each with about 30 residents. There have been many other attempts at developing cohousing but, for a host of reasons, most have failed. Perhaps because the intentional community movement in Australia is so rural-focused, people are less interested in urban alternatives?

Danthonia, Australia's first Bruderhof, is located near Inverell in rural New South Wales. It was founded in 1999 and now has about 50 residents with approved plans to grow to 400. They faced stiff opposition from some conservative neighbours who feared, among other things, that a nasty American 'cult' was being established in their midst. In general, the local council backed the Bruderhof and, after an expensive and time-consuming exercise, full development approval has been granted. They are on very good agricultural land, which they farm, although their main income will probably derive from the same light industrial base as described in the next chapter for American and British Bruderhofs.

Some of Australia's best known intentional communities are: Bodhi Farm, Bundagen, Dharmananda, New Govardhana and Tuntable Falls, in New South Wales; The Wolery, in Western Australia; Commonground and Moora Moora, in Victoria; Cennednyss, in South Australia; and Chenrezig, Crystal Waters, Magnificat Meal and Mandala, in Queensland. Most of these began during the early to mid 1970s, so they now have ageing memberships with a great deal of intentional community wisdom and experience. They range in size from about 6 to 300 people, have environmental, spiritual and humanistic orientations, and generally fit well into their environment and neighbourhood. Because most of them have failed to retain their children or attract other young people as members, their futures may become problematic through an ageing membership. The Wolery is described in detail in the next chapter.

∞∞∞

With the possible exception of Israel, the intentional community is healthy and growing around many parts of the globe. The three most popular forms of new intentional communities are cohousing, ecovillages and communes based on new religious movements. With the exception of new religious groups, the trend is that new groups are less radical than would have been the case 30 years ago, and most existing intentional communities are becoming less communal. One can lament this as a sad loss of utopian, communal fervour, or accept it as 'developmental communalism' wherein groups adjust to new personal, economic and political realities.

I have mentioned many of the long-lasting intentional communities but it must be admitted that they are a small minority and today, as throughout history, most groups have short lives. It is important to remember, however, that intentional communities have about the same longevity, with a similar turnover of members, as found in other social institutions. Ben Zablocki, an American researcher, reported in *Alienation and Charisma* that 'commune membership turnover is high but not extraordinarily high compared with that of other organizations. … Hospital nurses and factory workers both turnover a bit faster than commune members. University professors, civil servants, and prison wardens … a bit more slowly'. Three decades of research around the globe leads me to believe that this pattern is roughly universal, except for the Israeli kibbutzim and certain religious groups such as the Hutterites and Bruderhof.

Again with the above exceptions, while it appears that roughly half of intentional communities collapse within the first two or three years, and perhaps half the remainder have collapsed after about five years, roughly the same is found for small business ventures such as cafés, bookshops and and IT firms. Intentional communities are created by humans, with all our human foibles, and they are often unstable and impermanent—but so too are most other human creations. Remember also that many intentional communities survive and prosper for many generations.

In the next chapter I describe eleven intentional communities which exemplify these issues.

Chapter 5

INTENTIONAL COMMUNITY WORD PICTURES

INTRODUCTION

In this chapter, I present case studies of eleven intentional communities in different parts of the world. I selected these to give geographical breadth, and to represent the range of intentional communities. I selected these groups because I know them well, and I know that I can offer insights based on my long acquaintance with each one. I am not suggesting that these are the only groups I could have presented nor that they are necessarily 'better' than other groups.

In each word picture, I try to help readers understand the core issues of intentional community life such as governance, degree of communality, economic management and dealing with dissent. I then use these eleven small case studies as examples when discussing issues of intentional community life in Chapter Seven.

I provide contact information for each group. If one wishes to visit a group, make contact as far as possible in advance. Several of them have extensive facilities for guests, and Findhorn Foundation, ZEGG, Lothlorien and Damanhur have guest programs as part of their outreach. It is important to bear in mind that intentional communities are not charitable institutions and that one must normally contribute in some way to the costs of being a guest. Most importantly, never just show up unannounced at the doorway/gateway!

1. COMMUNITY ALTERNATIVES, CANADA

While most intentional communities in this section are rural, Community Alternatives has a large urban base between Vancouver's city centre and university, and a small rural base. The well-educated, middle class members live within a large, purpose-built timber structure, surrounded by organic gardens. In some ways, it is a blend of commune and cohousing, demonstrating how intentional community can be modified to suit a broad range of people and tastes. I have twice visited this urban/rural intentional community and still have friendly contacts there.

This community began in 1977 when several dedicated people met to establish an ideal society: non-sexist, intergenerational, cooperative, egalitarian and governed by consensus. By 1979, they had pooled money and obtained finance to build their 100-room communal house. As well as large common areas, it is divided into apartments which they call 'pods', three with eight bedrooms, two with four bedrooms and four with three bedrooms. Each pod has a kitchen, lounge and toilets. Members eat most meals within their pod. Pods determine how communal or independent they are, with some sharing resources and all meals within a pseudo family setting, while others comprise little more than individuals who share space and an occasional meal.

The community's eight-hectare (twenty-acre) farm is 'Fraser Common' to the east of the city. The original idea was to enjoy the best of both rural and urban living although this has not really worked out. Today, twenty-nine adults and eleven children live in town while nine adults and two children live on their farm. Members have no unified religious or political direction although most would admit to some form of ecospirituality. Some members stay for only a short time while others have been there almost since the beginning. While the city population is stable, the rural group is growing and has recently opened a second residence.

Most decisions are taken within pod groups. Farm and city residents meet at least monthly to discuss and decide on larger issues. All residents and many non-residential supporters belong to Community Alternative Society, the legal entity which holds title to, and is financially responsible for, all property and other assets. Over the years, members have had many disputes but have learned to use consensus decision-making to achieve win-win outcomes. They have no fall-back position should consensus fail.

They are interested in community economics, appropriate technology, alternate family forms, meaningful employment, collective social action and consensus decision-making, although I feel their commitment has slipped. The recent replacement of several long term members by younger people may mean that lessons need to be re-learned.

To join, a person pays C$1500 (US$1000 or £650), plus a monthly fee of C$300-500 (US$200-330 or £130-220) in the city and C$300 (US$200 or £130) on the farm. As well, members contribute for food within their pod, and are expected to do a certain amount of community work such as gardening, cleaning or maintenance.

Kaz Takahashi, a long term Community Alternatives member, tells me they now have 'occasional potlucks [communal dinners] whereas in the past they were weekly. Celebrations of birthdays are held. Meetings of the whole have dwindled to one a month instead of two or three.' More positively, she notes 'we have a small core of newer, younger folks who appear to want to stay and continue the legacy of the group. Most of the oldtimers have gone and the torch has to be carried on by younger people so a concerted effort is now made to have committed young folks join.' She adds, however, that the community has 'changed in attitude', and she is concerned about 'the lack of commitment to intentional [community] living'.

Several years back Jan Bulman, a friend of mine and one of Community Alternatives' founders, wrote in my book, *Shared Visions, Shared Lives*:

> *We have fine musicians, singers and song writers who enliven our gatherings. For ten years a 35 member gospel choir group which included several of our members … filled the place with song Monday nights. We're an easy bunch to party with. My courtyard retirement party with a live, mostly in-house band was unforgettable!*
>
> *If this sounds like a little bit of heaven, well it is.*
>
> *Not that it's all constantly heaven on earth. Anyone living with more than just her/himself knows the ups and downs, agonies and ecstasies that go along with group living, but it's lively.*

∞∞∞

I love Community Alternatives and hope one day, far hence, to die here.

That passion no longer seems to be so obviously present at Community Alternatives, and it may be significant that Jan has left to join Windsong Cohousing.

Like all long-term intentional communities, Community Alternatives has been flexible enough to adapt to changing cultural, political, social and economic realities. It is dangerous for any intentional community to be inflexible. But too much flexibility can also be a problem, and intentional communities can find themselves becoming ever less of a radical alternative and ever more of just a pleasant (or even unpleasant!) neighbourhood. I see this as a potential problem for Community Alternatives as it appears to have lost some of its original zeal and radical drive. Over the next few years, will it regain its radical direction and again be a force for equality, justice and environmental sustainability, or will it devolve into a pleasant apartment complex?

✍ Contact: Community Alternatives Co-op, 1937 West 2nd Avenue, Vancouver, BC V6J-1J2, CANADA
Further Reading: Jan Bulman's article, 'Love-Puddlers and Social Activists'.

2. DAMANHUR, ITALY

When standing in a cavernous room, 40 metres underground in Damanhur's Temple of Humankind, one appreciates the power and energy of this amazing intentional community. Using hand tools and ceaseless toil, Damanhurians excavated this elaborate subterranean complex over many years—and work continues. Each room is elaborately decorated with a different theme. The walls of one room are inscribed with strange symbols based, I am told, on 'Selfic' science, using a language pre-dating all other languages and known only to Damanhurians.

Selfic science has 3 principles: as above, so below; similar responds to similar; and thoughts create reality. A small part of Selfica is alchemy which can transform the 'subtle energies' of a person, animal or thing into something else. Damanhurians believe that colours and metals have vibrations that affect health, so, for example, a Selfic copper bracelet ensures well-being. Selfica can be used only for good, never for personal gain nor to harm people.

Damanhur began in 1977 when Oberto Airaudi, known today as Falco, and several friends settled in the impoverished Valchiusella valley in north-western Italy. They sought to create an intentional community where they could pursue the study of esoterics, and live as they chose. Damanhur was sited where four 'synchronic lines' intersect. Synchronic lines, I am told, are 'energy rivers that surround the earth and link it to the universe. These energy flows are able to catalyse the great forces present in the cosmos. The lines can modify events and carry ideas, thoughts and moods, thereby influencing all living creatures.'

Damanhur is growing rapidly, with about 600 resident members plus 400 non-residents. Recognising the fact that child-rearing presents a high opportunity cost to any communal group, they try to plan births according to social and economic priorities. Damanhur's midwives deliver children at home. Damanhurian marriage contracts are for a mutually agreed time, and are renewable if both parties agree. Members live in one of 44 'nucleos' (communal households) of up to 25 adults and children, sharing household chores, child-rearing and meals.

Damanhurians have weekly meditation meetings as well as talks by their founder, business discussions and social events. Annually, they celebrate the Solstices and Equinoxes, as well as a 'Ritual of Dead', Damanhur's Spiritual Birthday, People's Day, and Beginning of Damanhurian Year. In their calendar, September 1, 2003 is New Year's Day of year 29.

Damanhur 'citizens', as they prefer to be called, select two 'Guides' who coordinate the Federation and make decisions in accordance with their Federation Council which is comprised of representatives of the nucleos, work departments, etc. Decisions are generally reached by consensus. Falco, their spiritual guide, doesn't have any special role in governance although Damanhurians obviously trust him and value his opinions. Damanhur has a constitution, its own complementary currency (the credito), daily newspaper, medical services, schools, university and bus service. In some ways Damanhur is like a small nation-state.

Libera Università di Damanhur (Free University of Damanhur) offers courses on Esoteric and Spiritual Physics, the Ancient and Futuristic Science of Selfica, True Nature of Time and Space, Structure of The Soul and Human Personality, Life, Death and Past Lives, Pranatherapy and Healing Techniques, Sacred Dance, Astral Travel and Auto-hypnosis and Creative Visualisation. They welcome collaboration with academic researchers from around the globe, with whom 'the results of over twenty years of experimentation at Damanhur are open'.

In Damanhurian spiritual science, time is not linear 'conventionally going from past to future, but also a temporal sea of constant present, where all events are present contemporaneously'. Time travel, they believe, can take us only into the past, and 'it is important to keep the door open in order to be able to return'.

Damanhur has about 60 communally owned businesses including Atelier Damjl (high fashion accessories), Compagnia della Buona Terra (exclusive organic produce), and Cyber Damanhur (regional internet provider). Some members work outside of these communal businesses. My Damanhurian friend, Lepre Viola, tells me their

> *economic system is fundamentally based on the idea of SHARING. In Damanhur's philosophy "work" has a wide meaning: It is a means to provide for material needs and to produce shared wealth. Through work, every Damanhurian builds a part of his/her social and spiritual accomplishments, directed towards the common good.*

As part of the Global Ecovillage Network, Damanhurians seek to provide and use environmentally sustainable food, housing and energy technology. Eco-Damanhur Association is now a major Italian player in this field and is developing an international reputation.

Damanhur's creativity and industry have helped transform an impoverished region into an economic miracle. Several Damanhurians are on the local government council and one member was recently elected as mayor. Relations between Damanhurians and their neighbours are good in spite of occasional concerns by some non-Damanhurians that they are being taken over by their communal neighbours.

People wishing to join Damanhur spend six months in their Cento Cittadini (Introduction) program, living and working within the community. At the end of this training, if deemed suitable, they can become citizens. Members vow to 'follow the laws of Damanhur and the natural laws of good communal living and engage in the work of Damanhur'.

Damanhur's spiritual system is esoteric and hard to grasp. Professor Massimo Introvigne, in the *Encyclopedia of Community* (pp. 111-2), writes that Damanhurians believe:

> *God is accessible only through a group of lesser deities, the intermediate deities. … Not to be confused with the intermediate deities are beings called entities, which include angels, nature spirits, and demons. According to Damanhur's cosmological scheme, which derives heavily from Theosophy, the first human is described as a primeval deity, who was the victim of a fall and lapsed into the present union with the body. Many deities and entities voluntarily followed the humans into their exile and now help humans who try to return to their original, 'subtler' state.*
>
> *Damanhur's cosmology includes … three Mother worlds 'the world of human beings, the world of plants, and the world of nature spirits'. … Each … has an astral … repository of all knowledge accumulated … during the whole course of its history. … Human beings may get in touch … with the human race mind … but they may find very useful information also in the race minds of animals.*

This is why most Damanhurians adopt the names of animals and plants with whom they feel spiritually connected, such as Gorilla Eucalipto (Gorilla Eucalyptus), Orango Riso (Orang-utan Rice) and Esperide Ananas (Butterfly Pineapple).

Damanhur is incredibly successful in the financial, social and cultural fields. More than 50,000 visitors come each year to this major tourist attraction. Visitors are welcome at their Guest House, restaurants and workshops. Damanhur is one of the most interesting intentional communities in the world, regularly interacting with other communities such as ZEGG, Auroville and Findhorn Foundation. Damanhur's website states that they are 'an internationally renowned center for spiritual, artistic and social research. Damanhur is a school of thought that has given life to a new society and a new People; a way of living and thinking that has become an inspiration for the whole planet.'

Damanhur's economic, social and cultural achievements offer an inspirational model of intentional community. Damanhurians are intelligent, friendly and passionate about intentional community life, and always open to change. My admiration is not diminished by my scepticism about their esoteric claims.

✍ Contact: Federazione di Damanhur, Via Pramarzo 3, 10080 Baldissero Canavese (TO) ITALY
Web site: http://www.damanhur.org
Email: welcome@damanhur.it
Further Reading: Jeff Merrifield's book, Damanhur: *The Real Dream.*

3. DARVELL BRUDERHOF, ENGLAND

Darvell Bruderhof is south of London, on 120 hectares (296 acres) of farm land, near the site of the famous Battle of Hastings of 1066. Their ancient Manor House is surrounded by apartment style residences, a school, factory and large dining hall. Although technologically very modern, in some ways Darvell reminds me of a medieval village community.

The Bruderhof began in Germany in 1920 when Eberhard and Emmy Arnold formed a small commune at Sannerz, near Fulda. During the 1930s, they were persecuted by the Nazis, so the community moved to England, then, during World War Two, to Paraguay. Following a major crisis, they moved to USA in the early 1960s where they grew rapidly. There are now eleven Bruderhof communities in USA, Australia, Germany and UK. They are part of the Anabaptist tradition (as are Amish, Hutterites and Mennonites) believing in pacifism, Christian socialism and communal living 'like the first Christians in Jerusalem (see Acts 2 and 4 in the Bible), sharing everything except our spouses'. Women usually wear modest 'peasant' dresses and head scarves, while men wear dark clothes and beards. Members move between Bruderhof communes on different continents as the need arises.

Darvell was established in 1971 and now has about 300 communards. Members sometimes have large families, so almost half of the residents are children. Families live in apartments where they eat breakfast, while all other meals are taken in the dining hall. Women prepare the food while men serve and clean up. Children are the ultimate responsibility of the entire community although parents take primary responsibility for the ongoing guidance and nurture of each child. Children attend primary school within the community, then go to the local high school where their distinctive dress no longer draws much attention. While at Darvell, I spoke with several young people who were being supported to undertake university and technical training.

Not surprisingly, they found it a challenge to balance academic study in a big city university or college social environment with the demands of religious communal life.

Justin Peters, a Bruderhof friend of mine, tells me:

> *Single members of the Bruderhof do not date. If a young man falls in love with a young woman, he first tells the Elder of the Bruderhof about it. If the Elder feels that this young man and this young woman will lead each other closer to a true discipleship of Jesus, through a relationship of love, he gives his permission for them to write letters to each other, not love letters, but letters about what is important to them spiritually. We believe that a marriage which is not built on firmly held and shared Christian convictions will not stay together long. First there must be communion of spirit, then of emotions, and only then of bodies. Sexual activity outside of marriage is sin. The Bruderhof is ready to accept any repentant sinner into our midst, but we cannot accept a person continuing in a sinful relationship, whether heterosexual or homosexual.*

Although part of the multinational Bruderhof, Darvell has considerable autonomy. Adults meet regularly to discuss community issues and any member can block a decision. They choose an administrative committee to make day to day decisions. For major issues affecting all Bruderhofs, they communicate by telephone until consensus can be reached. Members are 'expected to speak out if she or he feels that a decision does not reflect the mission of the church, or is opposed on conscientious grounds'.

Some critics accuse the Bruderhof of sexism although this is certainly not how members see it. Justin tells me 'we feel that women's and men's intrinsic qualities are neither identical nor interchangeable but that they are equal in value. There are precious qualities which are only to be found in women, and precious qualities which are only to be found in men.'

Membership is open to anyone who feels 'personally called by God; this allows a person to sacrifice all kinds of personal preferences, career goals, etc.' Applicants correspond with a Bruderhof member, then visit. If accepted, they join for a probation period before final acceptance. Membership is for life and members are very critical of anyone who changes his/her mind.

Community Playthings is a Bruderhof owned company which produces wooden toys for children, and equipment for the physically challenged. This is Darvell's main employment and source of income. All income belongs to the collective and all expenses are shared. Members can have spending money, as needed. Their cars and trucks are available for private use although frivolous trips are discouraged. Darvell members appear to be prosperous and comfortable, although no doubt consuming far less than their neighbours. Overall funds are controlled by all Bruderhof communities working in concert so that, for example, large amounts could be marshalled for expansion into Australia and Germany. Should Darvell face financial problems it would be supported by the other communes.

I see Darvell and the other ten Bruderhofs as having three potential problems:

1) They only have one significant source of income, leaving them financially vulnerable.

2) Their high birthrate puts a strain on their resources. In my opinion, while being environmentally responsible and frugal in many ways, their refusal to curb their population probably works against their recognition as responsible global citizens. Bruderhof members disagree with my opinion on this.

3) The Bruderhof have evoked a strong, antagonistic response from some former members who publish a newsletter called KIT (Keep In Touch), harshly picturing the Bruderhof as a wicked, dictatorial cult. Having stayed several days at Darvell, and visited two other Bruderhofs, I have not witnessed the alleged abuses. Nevertheless, these strident attacks dog the Bruderhof.

Darvell comprises hard-working and dedicated Christian communards who work and live within the modern world while maintaining their socialist and pacifist principles. I respect and admire their social work with prisoners, and their anti-war activities. Their communal factories outperform the competition, and they demonstrate that communal economics works. Darvell is a thriving, spiritually-based intentional community.

✍ Contact: Darvell Bruderhof, Robertsbridge, TN32 5DR, East Sussex, ENGLAND
Web page: http://www.bruderhof.com
email: info@bruderhof.com
Further Reading: Ulrich Eggers' book, *Community for Life.*

4. THE FINDHORN FOUNDATION, SCOTLAND

Beyond a doubt, Findhorn Foundation is the best known intentional community in the world. Numerous books and extensive media coverage, in many languages, have ensured that Findhorn Foundation is the model to which many other intentional communities aspire, and against which many others are compared. Findhorn Foundation's spiritual doctrines and practices led one wit to call it 'The Green Party at Prayer'.

This community began in 1962 when Eileen and Peter Caddy, with their children and their friend Dorothy Maclean, moved onto a Caravan Park on an ugly stretch of sand near Findhorn village. All three adults were on highly disciplined, esoteric spiritual paths, and had years of training and practice. Eileen, when meditating, received messages from God, also called 'The Still Small Voice Within', while Dorothy received messages from the 'Nature Kingdoms'. Peter, the epitome of positive thinking, had absolute faith in these messages and acted upon them without hesitation. Soon they developed a healthy garden, visitors started arriving and a ramshackle community developed with everyone crowded into a few old caravans. As word spread, numbers grew rapidly, the community prospered and they bought not only the caravan park but several large buildings including the nearby Cluny Hill Hotel. By the mid 1980s, Findhorn Foundation's 300 members shared most meals, depended on their communal economy, and lived largely under centralised control.

Since then, they have been decentralising and privatising so that Findhorn Foundation's staff members have shrunk to under 100 while a loose but committed community of perhaps 500 others surround and help support the Foundation. These supporters, some of whom are employees, are financially independent, with some of them running businesses which formerly belonged to the Foundation. Staff members' ages range from mid 20s to 70s while the larger community includes all age groups. Most members of both groups are well educated and highly skilled. Residential staff members receive a monthly allowance plus food and housing.

Within Findhorn Foundation, staff members work in areas such as kitchen, gardens, homecare, maintenance, education, guests and administration. Most decisions are reached within those work groups. Larger matters are discussed within a Management Committee of senior members, and some issues are referred to the entire community where decisions are generally reached by consensus. There is a newly formed Findhorn Foundation Council, a consultative and advisory group, comprising a wide range of members. Overall, a Board of Trustees is legally and financially responsible, and occasionally has to make important decisions—although rarely going against the wishes of the community.

Most staff members live in Foundation accommodation and eat in large dining rooms at their two main sites, The Park and Cluny Hill College. The 20 to 30 staff staying in Cluny live within a gracious, 140 year old stone building which can also accommodate over 100 guests. The ballroom alone is larger than many houses. Those in The Park live in caravans, bungalows or newly built, eco-friendly housing. Some members of the wider community rent Foundation housing while some staff live in their own houses. Some of their organic food is grown within their gardens with more coming from an associated Earthshare organic farming scheme. They produce a significant amount of electricity from their wind generator, and most human wastes are treated in their 'Living Machine'. Ecological sustainability is an important part of their mission.

Findhorn Foundation's educational programs and guest accommodation charges bring in most of their income. The rest comes from rent and donations. The wider community members have a broad range of income sources from computer businesses, pensions, holistic health, consultancy, Phoenix Store, bakery, Findhorn Press, farming, etc. These 500 or so people often donate time and money to the Foundation and are staunch supporters of Foundation activities.

Meditation is central to community life. The 'Sanctuaries' or meditation rooms at Cluny Hill College and The Park are the focus of spiritual life—while the dining rooms are the focus of social life. Work groups regularly meditate together, and most important community decisions are reached only after meditation. Through meditation, they believe they contact a greater wisdom which clarifies issues and suggests solutions. Some believe this to come from some external, God-like entity while others see this wisdom as having come from within. In either event, meditation is an important community bonding and conflict resolution mechanism.

To join Findhorn Foundation, one attends an Experience Week, then their Living in Community Program. The final stage is to undertake a 3-12 month probation program, after which the person is eligible to apply for a staff position. People generally stay less than a decade although there are some members of 30+ years standing and one of the founders, Eileen Caddy, still lives there.

A wide range of educational and experiential programs are offered, ranging from holistic health and sexuality to international conferences. Four thousand people annually attend their courses, with another 10,000 visitors coming just to look around. Findhorn College offers accredited university level programs, while their Ecovillage Training Program is recognised by the Global Ecovillage Network. As well as education and meditation, guests and members enjoy a rich and diverse cultural life including music, sacred dance, art, pottery and theatre. Every time I visit, there is more to do than I can handle. In the dining room, one chats with people from around the globe and from a wide diversity of backgrounds. Members joke that they are not as isolated as maps suggest because the world comes to Findhorn.

One of Findhorn Foundation's main functions has been to train thousands of people from around the globe in intentional community living. This was not the original intent of the founders but may be its greatest achievement. As part of the Global Ecovillage Network, this aspect of Findhorn Foundation's mission increases. Two major associated projects, The Field of Dreams and Dunelands, are allowing even more people to build ecological houses there. Some people now see the community as something like a medieval village surrounding and supporting a monastery.

In 1997, Findhorn Foundation was recognised by the United Nations as an official Non-Governmental Organisation. Since then, they have been accredited to participate in several international conferences including Habitat 2 and Earth Summit. This U.N. recognition helps move Findhorn Foundation onto a whole new level of global interaction.

When I first stayed at Findhorn Foundation in 1982, it was almost the total intentional community, everyone worked for and was financially dependent on it, with centralised control. Today, Findhorn Foundation is still by far the biggest financial and social entity but contains less than 20% of the members of the wider community. This development can be either seen as bad—with the original intentional community having been swamped by non-members—or good, an example of 'Developmental Communalism' whereby the original communal group changed and developed new models to meet new needs. The reality is that whether good or bad, to survive, all intentional communities, like all other social forms, must change and adapt to new circumstances, including the ageing of members. Not to change is to die—the fate of so many erstwhile intentional communities. Along with many older members, however, I fear that their core spiritual values and social mission may be slipping—but that does not detract from Findhorn Foundation's significance as one of the world's great intentional communities.

At Findhorn Foundation's 40th birthday celebrations, Dorothy Maclean, one of the co-founders, said 'we were trying to follow the wishes of the divine. That a community of hundreds of people, visited by thousands more would result is an incredible, awesome miracle. After forty years the loving magic we helped ground at Findhorn is still doing its work.'

✍ Contact: The Findhorn Foundation, The Park, Forres IV36 3TZ, SCOTLAND
Web page: http://www.findhorn.org
Email: enquiries@findhorn.org
Further Reading: Karin Bogliolo & Carly Newfeld's book, *In Search of the Magic of Findhorn.*

5. KADARIM, ISRAEL

Kadarim is a kibbutz, part of one of the most fascinating aspects of the global intentional community movement. About an hour's drive north west of Haifa, perched high on a rocky plateau overlooking the Sea of Galilee (Lake Kinneret), Kadarim offers sweeping views of the biblical 'Promised Land'. Their housing is modest but carefully laid out to enjoy the views, while lawns and shade trees offer a welcome respite from the intense Galilean sun.

Kadarim members, while ethnically Jewish, and celebrating religious festivals, are not particularly religious. They live in community not to practice Judaism but to realise their dream of communal living within a free Israel.

Most kibbutzniks have leftist backgrounds and many have been involved for years in peace activism.

About 50 adults and 50 young people comprise Kadarim's population. Many members have come from Australia, New Zealand and USA, so English as well as Hebrew are spoken. Because Kadarim is only 23 years old, adults tend to be in their late 20s to late 40s, suggesting a potentially serious age imbalance in another 20-30 years.

Members are elected to a Secretariat which manages their daily business and finances. All members can take part in monthly general assemblies. Several times each year, when a big issue/problem looms, members hold an intensive forum at which all aspects can be examined and discussed, feelings aired and, hopefully, consensus achieved.

Traditionally within kibbutzim, everything except personal effects belong to the collective. Starting in the mid 1990s, Kadarim members started moving toward greater personal autonomy. While education and health care are still paid for by the collective, most other expenses are the responsibility of the individual. About 40% of Kadarim's income is now distributed to members. Even the houses are being legally transferred to members who live therein, meaning that this asset can be sold or inherited when a member leaves or dies.

When asked how these changes fit with his strong communal drive, Garry Favel, a Kadarim friend of mine, says 'I don't feel like we sold out, what was good for us when we were 22 was not what we wanted when 32, and now at 42 we want to own our houses. We are evolving, and the community continues to grow and thrive and be full of relatively happy people who are proud of what they have built and achieved.'

Kadarim owns several businesses, the most important being Kapro, manufacturing top quality spirit levels and other precision measuring instruments. Other communal businesses include a chicken farm, a 30 room accommodation and conference centre, a mango grove and a citrus orchard. About 15 members work within these businesses while others work off site in professions such as teacher, nurse and consultant, with all wages going to Kadarim. While many kibbutzim have faced financial crises over the past decade, Kadarim remains relatively prosperous and secure.

In most kibbutzim, members eat most meals together but at Kadarim this only happens on Friday nights (Shabbat), and on other Jewish holidays. They have their own pub, and a band which plays at regional events. Members often travel together for social events such as hiking, and the entire group annually spends a weekend together at the beach. When I stayed at Kadarim, I noticed a great deal of social interaction between members. I attended a child's birthday party, at which most members were present, and drank beer with some of my fellow Australians who were listening to Aussie Rules football. I found the atmosphere to be relaxed and socially cohesive.

Potential members stay as guest workers for six months then, if accepted, enter a year long probation period after which they can become full members by a two-thirds majority vote. Kadarim is looking for new members, particularly young families

Garry Favel tells me, 'I am very happy, love my family, job, friends, life is great' but then adds, 'I hope our community will grow … we must make sure that we have a critical mass to ensure our services can keep running. I assume my kids will want to travel, but hopefully they will come and live here or nearby. I see myself here for the long haul, we are committed, but work now to ensure that when we get to 65 years old, in say 20 years, we will have a community of perhaps 300 adults.' Ruth Lacey, another Kadarim friend of mine, doubts that this would be possible or wise, fearing the destabilising social impacts and ecological damage from growing so fast.

Any discussion of intentional community in Israel must address the peace process and the Palestinian situation. Kadarim's dining room overlooks several Palestinian villages and, if the weather is clear, the contested Golan Heights, near Syria. Fortunately, Kadarim has been spared the inter-ethnic violence which has occurred in many other parts of the country. When I ask Garry about this he says:

> *Over the past 2-3 years I have become more right wing than ever, I still want peace but am sceptical of the Palestinian leadership's ability or desire to reach peace. Never thought I would wait for George Bush to come over and save us, and Yasser Arafat, and force us into an agreement, but it seems like the only way. We may get forced into an agreement, but the spirit will not be there immediately, it will take time.*

Kadarim is certainly different from Degania, the first kibbutz of almost a century ago, but it provides a lesson. In any intentional community, members must adapt to changes within their own lives and within the wider world—but they must still respect the fundamental values which underpin their reasons for communal living or else there is no point to the exercise. At this stage, it appears as if Kadarim is managing to walk this tight rope and their future appears bright.

✍ Contact: Kibbutz Kadarim, D.N. Bikat Bet Hakerem, 12390, ISRAEL.
Web site: http://www.kadarim.org.il
Email: kadarim@kadarim.org.il
Further Reading: Daniel Gavron's book, *The Kibbutz: Awakening from Utopia.*

6. KOMMUNE NIEDERKAUFUNGEN, GERMANY

Kommune Niederkaufungen is in a complex of beautiful, centuries-old 'Fachwerk' farm buildings and manor house near Kassel. The large dining and lounge areas, with adjoining courtyard, are the focus of communal life.

In 1986, a group of dedicated Germans, seeking to live communally, established Kommune Niederkaufungen. They had no religious or spiritual base, but believed in equality, socialism and environmentalism. According to their website:

> *we wanted to prove that a group of committed people is able to financially survive within capitalist society without having to surrender to the seemingly unchangeable and sometimes barbaric rules of the system. We didn't want to create our unspoiled little island in the middle of nowhere … but rather aimed at setting up collectively run businesses which produce for the market as well as for community-needs.*

Today, 72 people, ranging from babies to early 50s, enjoy a comfortable communal life. Members have private rooms within ten 'living groups' of three to ten adults, plus children. Each group has a living room and bathroom, and meet as needed for discussions. Everyone eats together in the large, comfortable dining room. Several members, mostly male, cook main meals during the week, while members are rostered to prepare breakfasts and weekend meals. Members rarely change jobs, unlike most other communal groups, allowing the development of an experienced and efficient work force.

They operate under six principles seeking: a broad, shared economy; consensus decision-making; a flexible, left-wing political attitude; reduction of nuclear-family structures; gender equality; and an ecological approach to work and life. One of their practical goals is to reduce air travel as much as possible because of its intensive energy use.

Members belong to one of eleven work areas: carpentry, seminar centre, construction, kitchen, organic gardening, dairy farm, leatherwork, architecture, public kindergarten, metalwork, administration/consulting. Within each group, members agree on working hours, vacations, setting prices and ecological standards. Kommune Niederkaufungen has no employees, 'we want no bosses and we don't want to become bosses' they tell me. Each work area reports annually to a meeting of all communards. All profits from work areas go into the common purse. Their weekly plenum also discusses community-wide matters such as accepting a new member, major investments, and policy interpretations, with decisions made by consensus. Twice yearly, all members participate in a three day retreat to examine where they are going, if fundamental changes are needed, discuss their guiding philosophy, etc. Several members work off-site, with their income going into the common purse.

Their guest house and conference centre can cater for 30 people at a time, bringing money into the community and helping Kommune Niederkaufungen become better known. As well, guests who are interested in joining the commune can visit and stay for a very low cost, but must make contact before arriving. Members are particularly anxious to interact with people from intentional communities around the globe, but only where this can be done with minimal environmental costs, and without air travel if at all possible.

Their businesses are reasonably successful, earning enough to meet communal living costs of about €50,000 (US$55,000; £35,000) per month which includes food, housing, cars, clothes, books, health-insurance, telephone, cigarettes, beer, chocolate, ice-cream, holiday-trips, etc. As well, they donate a considerable amount to various environmental and peace causes, and help establish and sustain other intentional communities. I have stayed twice at Kommune Niederkaufungen, finding that they live a comfortable lifestyle with great meals. Their comfortable yet frugal lifestyle does not result from doing without but from sharing resources. For example, 70 people share seven cars, two washing-machines and two video-recorders. When members need money for personal matters, they simply take it from a box of cash which sits in their office. They do not ask anyone's approval, but record how it will be used: toiletries, cinema, travel, etc. These expenses are displayed at the end of each month, tallied according to how the money was spent but not by who spent it. Trust and honesty are crucial. This system works remarkably well although occasionally discussions arise in community meetings.

To join, a person attends an information weekend after which she/he can stay another week in order to find three or four members to be sponsors. After writing out a lengthy application about his/her interests, history and financial position, she/he may start a probation period of at least three months. After this, the person is eligible to apply for membership, but each existing member has a veto. If finally accepted, new members turn over all assets and debts to the collective which decides how these are to be handled. There is no joining fee, as such. If a member leaves, the group provides financial, emotional and practical support. Departing members receive what they need, which could be less or more than they brought in. Within Kommune Niederkaufungen, the only private property are clothes and personal effects. Membership is stable with several original members still there and most others staying at least a decade.

Most intentional communities which survive for the long term adhere to some form of spirituality. While Kommune Niederkaufungen claims to be non-spiritual, it is obvious to me that their humanist, socialist and ecological aims have an almost spiritual dimension. Members believe they have a mission to promote communal living, to be a model of co-operation, equality, equity and productivity, and to do what they can to promote world peace and environmental sustainability. This is the glue which holds them together and gives a common purpose.

I do not see any serious problems for Kommune Niederkaufungen. Their original members are still early middle-aged, and many young people wish to join, giving a fairly balanced age distribution—although lacking older people. They have a diverse income base, and their well-educated and highly skilled members have shown themselves flexible enough to adapt to economic changes. In many ways, they are like the Israeli kibbutzim of 20-30 years ago but so far they have avoided the trend to privatisation which has so altered kibbutzim and other well-known intentional communities. Members hope that Kommune Niederkaufungen will support them in their old age but they have also established a Community Pension Fund.

Members proudly proclaim, 'we have put many of our original ideas into reality. Some disillusionment was inescapable (we still know the difference between work and leisure time), some naiveté was lost (to work collectively doesn't in itself make you happy), but … we're making it happen each day right in the heart of the beast. It is possible!'

On a more personal note, Monika Flörchinger, a friend of mine at Kommune Niederkaufungen, tells me:

> *I can live in harmony with my values and needs. I like the possibilities and challenges for personal growth I find here, living in such a big reliable group. Most of all, I like it that we have a big common vision: to develop our ability to deal with each other in a respectful way. At the moment I have the picture for my future that I will stay here until the end of my life. But who knows what will happen in the future?*

✍ Contact: Kommune Niederkaufungen, Kirchweg 1, D-34260 Kaufungen, Germany
Web site: http://www.kommune-niederkaufungen.de
Email: kommune@t-online.de
Further Reading: Sven Borstelmann's article, 'Kommune Niederkaufungen'

7. LOTHLORIEN, BRAZIL

Imagine a small valley in South America with lush tropical vegetation, running streams and an almost perfect climate—and you have an image of Lothlorien.

In 1982, four middle-class professionals started Lothlorien community in Bahia state, northern Brazil. Lothlorien, meaning 'Golden Dream', derives from Tolkien's *The Lord of the Rings*. Lothlorien's four founders purchased 16 hectares (40 acres) of land where they sought to live their dream based on three principles: 1. Working on their own land, and planting gardens and fruit trees according to organic gardening principles; 2. Practising natural medicine and healthy eating habits; and 3. Practising 'unconditional love', to promote spiritual and emotional growth. The founders were strongly influenced by Findhorn Foundation's new-age philosophy and spiritual practice, and sought to make Lothlorien similar. A generation later, Lothlorien maintains its connections with Findhorn Foundation and still follows many of the same spiritual tenets and practices.

Members and long term guests meet weekly to discuss community business. Almost always, they manage to reach consensus but, if not, they will leave the issue until people have had a chance to think and discuss. Because of their small size and intense interactions, some form of consensus decision is always reached. For legal reasons, Lothlorien has a Board of Counsellors, comprised of past and present members and long-term supporters. They rarely interfere in daily community life but may offer guidance.

Lothlorien's communal income derives from workshops and structured holiday experiences for which they can cater for up to 30 guests at a time. Workshops range from new-age philosophy to natural healing and organic gardening. Full-time residents pay a monthly fee of R$40 (about US$12 or £8) to the collective. As well, everyone staying there does some community work, and contributes to the cost of food. Members are responsible for their own income and retain their own assets. Being somewhat isolated, it is difficult for Lothlorien members to earn outside income. Workshop and accommodation income is insufficient to meet all costs, so a shortage of money remains a problem for individuals and the collective, although their financial position is improving.

Early most days, members gather to practice yoga and meditation before breakfast. Typically, they work together all morning on whatever communal tasks they have agreed to do, then have a quick swim, before lunch in their communal dining room. Members work in the afternoons but also have time to do what they like. In the evening, they sometimes dine together, and occasionally socialise, but generally retire to their private space.

Lothlorien provides a health service and public library for local people. Members are politically active in many ways, working for the benefit of people within the wider community in fields such as education, health and environment.

They have five communal buildings: Communal House (kitchen, dining room, library and bathroom); House of Harmony (rooms for massage, medical assistance and office); Temple (for meditation, yoga, meetings and therapeutic work); Lodging House (for paying guests); and Nave (for people who come to share Lothlorien's communal life). As well, there are six family houses where permanent residents and some ex-members live.

Anyone wishing to join Lothlorien must stay for at least two months to get a feel for the place, and for members to form opinions about the applicant. If everyone is positive, then the person is accepted for a year's probation during which they have some but not all the rights and responsibilities of full members. At year's end, if all members and the Board of Counsellors agree, the person can become a full member.

In spite of their best efforts to grow, Lothlorien remains small. Their largest membership was about a dozen adults and nearly as many children. Today, only one of the founding members remains, along with three other adults, all middle-aged. They receive many young people who come to work with them for awhile and to learn about and take part in their spiritual and social life, but few stay.

I have known Lothlorien for a decade, during which they have faced a crisis or two, and had various problems, the most obvious being insufficient members to do the work, and to provide the social, intellectual and cultural diversity which seems to be essential to achieving happiness within an intentional community. That observation, however, begs the question of why more people have not become members. Their philosophical underpinning cannot be a problem because it certainly works very well elsewhere. Anyhow, while Lothlorien may have membership and financial problems—so too do most intentional communities. Perhaps they have had some bad luck in recruiting members—but then all communities have these problems.

Sonia Christophe, one of Lothlorien's founders, tells me:

According to Natural Medicine Philosophy, crises are to be considered positively as a sign that change is needed or is about to come. We've always come out of these crises stronger and more mature. And, although our financial situation is still "tight", my evaluation of our present situation is more positive than ever; we are fertile in new plans, projects and ideas and are working hard to put them into practice. Many other people are involved with Lothlorien and with our projects, maybe it's time to enlarge our conceptions of an intentional community to include all these people! I am still optimistic, but learning that things take some time to happen. ... Lothlorien is my golden dream, the project to which I still want to devote my life.

Lothlorien deserves to thrive and prosper because of the positive work they do within their physical environment and wider community, because of their international and Brazilian outreach work, and because of the wonderful people who are involved.

✍ Contact: Lothlorien - Centro de Cura e Crescimento, Caeté-Açu (Capão) 46.940-000 Palmeiras, Bahia, BRAZIL.
Website: http://www.lothlorien.org.br/english/
Email: centro@lothlorien.org.br
Further Reading: Sonia Christophe's chapter, *'A Brazilian Community in Crisis'.*

8. THE WOLERY, AUSTRALIA

With magnificent views over the Great Southern Ocean, a sandy beach within walking distance, eco-friendly housing and a well established group of mature residents, The Wolery is an impressive intentional community near the south coast of Western Australia. Most buildings cluster around their Community Centre in which meetings, communal meals and a wide range of social events take place. An intense feeling of community bonds is obvious here. During my visit, I notice that houses are rarely locked, children wander freely and safely between houses, and adults visit each other frequently to share garden produce, gossip, discuss community, national and international affairs, and help with menial tasks.

In 1977, several middle-aged, middle class people from an urban commune in Perth decided to pool their assets and move to the country to try to enjoy the advantages of urban commune living while avoiding the disadvantages. They purchased a 64-hectare (160-acre) abandoned dairy farm and lived in the old farm house while they designed and built separate houses.

They called themselves The Wolery, after the house of Wol, the owl who could not spell in Winnie the Pooh. They encountered some initial opposition from the local council who feared that they were being invaded by some drug-prone, sexually promiscuous cult but, through perseverance, they obtained legal permission to build their community.

The Wolery has a stable population of about 40 adults and children, living in 13 separate family houses and two special 'retirement units', mostly clustered around their Community Centre. The original members, of whom only two remain, were all involved in peace, social justice and environmental matters, and several had been members of the Communist Party. The Wolery today has no formal religious or political affiliations, although many members are actively involved in peace, green and social justice activism. Their relations with the local council and regional community appear to be warm and supportive. They serve as a model on which several other Australian intentional communities have been based.

Their large, attractive and comfortable Community Centre, made of rammed earth, has a massage room, large kitchen and dining area for community meals, meetings and social events, a bulk food store on the honour system, a children's play area plus video and TV room. A tennis court, sports field, and playground are nearby.

The Wols, as they call themselves, occasionally gather for a 'philosophy' meeting at which they discuss community issues but do not reach decisions. At subsequent monthly meetings, members make decisions, almost always by consensus. Where consensus is not possible yet a decision cannot be deferred, they accept a 75% majority vote. Decisions to admit a new member or change their constitution can be blocked by three dissenting members. During my visit, members assured me that they have not voted for years, with consensus almost always working. The physical layout of buildings, their frequent interactions, maturity, mutual respect and obvious affection probably explain why they have such an efficient form of communal governance.

At their annual general meeting, members are selected for the usual positions of Community Convenor, Secretary and Treasurer. Other members become Workshop Manager or the wittily entitled Minister for Cattle, Minister for the Tractor or Minister for Water. As far as possible, Wols try to include everyone while not allowing anyone to be isolated or dominating.

Almost all community income comes from members whose households each pay A$400 per annum (US$240 or £170), as well as a share of council rates. Members are responsible for their own incomes, with several being on retirement pensions, while others work from home as architects and information technologists, and still others work in and/or own businesses in the area. While not wealthy, The Wolery certainly gives me the feeling of enjoying environmentally-sensitive affluence.

Membership turnover is low but if a member leaves or dies, his/her house and share in The Wolery can be transferred to a new member, provided no more than three members disagree. The incoming member pays the departing member a negotiated amount for the house, but not the land (which always belongs to the collective) plus a A$10,000 (US$6000 or £4000), non-refundable fee to the community to compensate for previous investments in infrastructure. Before prospective members can join, they must visit all households to get to know members and gain their confidence. Their constitution has no provision to expel members because, as Enid Conochie, a founding member tells me, 'this was hotly debated in the early stages, but I argued strongly that if we wanted to encourage the feeling amongst members of belonging to a family, expulsion should not be an option.' I was assured that Wols have never regretted not having the power to expel one another.

Compared to many intentional communities, The Wolery has relatively few problems. The members and community appear to be reasonably financially secure and to get along remarkably well. Their membership is ageing although there is sufficient age distribution to make this not yet a big issue. While they are, in some ways, physically isolated in Western Australia, the nearby town of Denmark provides for their shopping, although not all cultural and intellectual needs. Anyhow, such isolation might be an asset?

While interacting often as an intentional community and sharing responsibility for the collective, the Wols enjoy personal independence. They obviously enjoy living in this great intentional community. In my opinion, The Wolery has a great future.

In 2002, when the Wols celebrated a quarter century as an intentional community, a young woman who grew up there but is now in Europe, wrote to say that she feels 'so proud to be even such a small part of such a place. I think when I was younger I took the safety, happiness and freedom for granted—as I knew nothing else—now, being away in other countries far across the sea I feel I can fully appreciate how lucky I was to have the pleasure of such a care-free childhood.' What a wonderful compliment!

✍ Contact: The Secretary, The Wolery, RMB 1050, Denmark, WA 6333, AUSTRALIA.
Email: conochie@denmarkwa.net.au
Further Reading: Enid Conochie's chapter, *'From Communism to Communalism'.*

9. TWIN OAKS, USA

Twin Oaks, in Virginia within 2½ hour's drive from Washington DC, is an impressive intentional community from which we can learn much because it was well planned and has roughly stuck to that plan for the past 36 years. The members are prosperous, dedicated and happy, contributing not only to the well-being of their region but also to the global intentional community movement. Their original four main values are income-sharing, non-violence, egalitarianism and cooperation, although one could now add environmentalism and feminism. To travel between Washington, DC, and Twin Oaks is a cultural and political odyssey, from hierarchical power and global domination to egalitarianism and environmental sustainability!

Twin Oaks started in 1967 when a group of people sought to live the ideal life as it had been described by the famous behavioural psychologist, B.F. Skinner in his book, *Walden Two*. Skinner believed that humans become whatever they are reared (socialised) and behaviourally rewarded to become. On the famous nature/nurture debate, Skinner was firmly in the latter camp. He believed that a community in which 'good' behaviour was rewarded had the ability to become almost utopian. The dedicated people who implemented this experiment in 1967 knew they would face many problems—but their success has been truly astonishing.

Twin Oaks now has about 90 adults and 15 children. The adults have a wide range of social and educational backgrounds, and range from early 20s to late 70s. Only one of the founders remains, although on long-term sabbatical, with members staying, on average, about a decade, before moving on.

Their governance is based on a Planner-Manager system combined with egalitarian values. Managers, chosen by members, are responsible for the daily work and decisions for areas such as kitchen, garden, outreach and for each business. For community-wide decisions on larger issues, the three Planners (serving 18-month terms) make decisions after looking at by-laws and actively soliciting community input, gathering information and determining the will of the community. Planners and Managers can be replaced at any time should they fail to attune to the common will, although this rarely happens.

Each year, the Managers and Planners propose an economic plan. Each member can alter the plan according to her/his values and preferences on how to spend their collective labour and money. Once members have done this, the Planners try to synthesise everyone's changes into a final work plan and budget for which everyone should feel responsible.

Members work within several communal businesses including making hammocks, indexing books and making tofu. These businesses earn sufficient money to pay all communal expenses and provide each member with food, clothing, health-care and housing, plus a personal allowance of US$75 (£50) per month. Members can apply for larger amounts for travel and holidays. They work 43 hours per week, including domestic chores such as cooking, laundry and child-care. Under their labour-credit system, all work has equal value, and most people work at several jobs. Work is chosen according to personal preferences but a Labour Assigner adjusts these to ensure that all needed work is completed. When I stayed at Twin Oaks, I was assigned to kitchen and cleaning, not because I was good at these but because they were the jobs needing more labour.

Each member has a private bedroom in one of eight large communal buildings. There is a modern dining room where meals (meat, vegetarian and vegan) are eaten together at midday and evening, and a lounge. Their organic gardens provide fresh food during the growing season, and dried, canned or frozen food for the rest of the year. Twin Oaks has a very active social life with weekly activities such as a choir, band, yoga class, juggling, knitting group, art workshop, scrabble night, video nights, women's and men's groups, and political discussion groups. As well, community-wide social activities such as dances, parties and games nights are held at least twice weekly.

Environmental concerns rate highly, with all vehicles being collectively owned and shared. Buildings have passive-solar heating, solar hot water is used throughout and one building is powered by solar-generated electricity.

Twin Oaks is always open to new members although their population is remarkably stable. They frequently offer a three week orientation program where participants work alongside community members, and attend orientation meetings. Anyone wishing to join is interviewed by the Membership Team. After three weeks, the prospective member must leave, and members share opinions and observations about her/him with the Membership Team which makes the final decision. New members can retain any personal assets but not use them. Any income from personal assets goes to the community. When a person leaves, they take their assets with them. Given the high cost of children, Twin Oaks allows only one child per five adults.

When I first visited Twin Oaks, they followed the kibbutz child-rearing model, with all children living together, reared collectively away from parents. Today, parents have responsibility for and live with their children. Those involved in child-care receive labor credits.

Valerie Renwick-Porter, a Twin Oaks member of eleven years, tells me:

> *Many people working for social justice use their energy to resist and struggle against the existing culture/governments/paradigms. My path is to lend my energy to the other part of the equation, to creating an alternative culture, working for, not against. Living at Twin Oaks is one of the best ways I know to do this, and I am grateful to have found this place, to live here, and to continue to create healthy, sustainable ways of being together on this planet.*

Valerie readily admits that Twin Oaks 'isn't Utopia yet', and 'there are things I wish were different here. [But] here I have more opportunities to actually influence the culture and actively create my environment.'

Having stayed at Twin Oaks, I wholeheartedly support her views.

✍ Contact Twin Oaks, 138 Twin Oaks Road, Louisa, VA 23093, USA
website: http://www.twinoaks.org
Email: twinoaks@ic.org
Further Reading: Kat Kinkade's book, *Is it Utopia Yet?*

10. WINDSONG COHOUSING, CANADA

Cohousing is a recent style of intentional community, attempting to enjoy the economic, environmental, social and cultural advantages of communal living while maintaining separate family dwellings, with members working and participating within mainstream society. Windsong, in British Columbia, nestles beneath the Rocky Mountains. Residents live together—but with privacy; act communally—but with little restraint on individuality; live environmentally sound lifestyles—but enjoy modern comforts. Many see this as living in intentional community without 'dropping out'.

Windsong started in 1991 when several people, some with intentional community experience, came together to explore a better way of life. In 1993, they purchased 2.5 hectares (6 acres) of semi-rural land along Yorkson Creek, an hour east of Vancouver. For three years, they worked closely with a professional cohousing adviser, architects and builders to create their ideal living environment into which they moved during July 1996. The total establishment cost was about C$5,200,000 (US$3,720,000 or £2,250,000).

From above, Windsong looks like an enormous, flat and strangely-shaped building with two large, glass-roofed areas. On the ground, the glassed areas are seen to be two atriums to which residential units and common facilities have access. Having only passive solar heating in the harsh Canadian winter, these atriums nevertheless promote social activity, allowing residents to be outside their individual living spaces while still within their collective, non-public space. Private entrances are marked with plants, rugs, and furniture 'like a strip of street cafés spilling onto the footpath'.

Windsong has about 60 adults and 35 children in 34 residential units of one to four bedrooms. Units have their own kitchen, toilet and lounge, and some have yards. Most members have middle-class, well-educated backgrounds and, according to their website, include an accountant, architect, business coach, chaplain (retired), consultant, civic worker, college instructor, doctor, electrician, farmer, film-maker, geologist, homemaker, journalist, librarian midwife, naturopath, nurse, nutritionist, office worker, physiotherapist, programmer, rolfer, salesperson, social worker, student, swim instructor, systems analyst, teacher, therapist, urban planner, waiter and x-ray technician!

At monthly meetings, members make, or just formalise, decisions which have emerged. Because of their extensive communication system with newsletters, notice boards and an intranet service, and because of physical proximity and frequent interactions, everyone knows about pending decisions and has time to seek information or raise objections. Members assume that since people are informed, unless they object they must accept the decision of the meetings. As with most consensus decision-making models, and since they have no fall-back position, decisions are often deferred to give people time to reconsider and negotiate win-win outcomes.

Windsong's communal facilities include a large kitchen and dining room, where members frequently eat together, a lounge for socialising, children's and teenager's rooms, craft area, workshop, laundry, office, and guest bedroom. There is a large community lawn and garden, and members may have their own gardens. Many communal meals are 'pot-lucks' to which residents donate food to be shared. On other nights, volunteers cook for everyone, often with a theme which might include songs, dancing or performance.

Windsong cohousing depends on fees of C$80 (US$54 or £34) to C$208 (US$140 or £88), per month from each household, depending on unit size. This maintains common facilities and equipment, and repays debt. Residents own their own housing units.

Members engage in social activities such as yoga, painting, tai chi, hiking and dancing. They have a book club, choir, creative writing and tennis groups. A high point of community life is the plays and revues performed on their dining room stage. Their commitment to intentional community ensures a rich cultural and social smorgasbord.

As with any cohousing group, members can sell their interest on the open market. This might appear to threaten the group, with non community-minded people joining, but this has not been the case. One member says, 'We explain to potential buyers that they are buying … a share in a community, not just a dwelling; that we manage the community ourselves and the expectation is that all residents will contribute in some way.' Units cost slightly more than conventional houses in the area but, although they are smaller, offer more facilities such as the small field, forest and salmon stream.

Windsong members seem happy with intentional community life. Gerry Kilgannon, a founding member, says:

> *The biggest advantage to living here is having a perfect balance between privacy and community. I say perfect, because I can determine the balance myself. I have my own space in which to spend as much time as I want and right outside my door is a variety of people to be with. We have the evening meal prepared once or twice a week by volunteer residents, for which we pay our share of the cost of ingredients. Otherwise we can choose to prepare our own meal or participate in a pot luck meal every other day or just take our own prepared dinner to the dining room and be in the company of others. We do many things together, such as gardening, cleaning the building, discussing books or other topics, going off-site to plays or concerts.*

I conclude with the observations of cohousing expert Dr Graham Meltzer:

> *At Windsong, high levels of interaction and social support, clear communication and efficient decision-making provide the conditions for a rich cultural life whereby members with talent, knowledge and skill freely share their gifts with others. The whole community benefits, whilst individuals and families have the opportunity to learn and grow profoundly.*

✍ Contact: Windsong, 20543, 96th Avenue, Langley BC, V1M3W3, CANADA. Website: http://www.cohousing.ca/cohsng4/windsong
Email: valandgreg@windsong.bc.ca (Valerie McIntyre)
Further Reading: Bruce McDougall's article, *'Going Green in the Burbs'*.

11. ZEGG, GERMANY

ZEGG is one of the best known intentional communities in the world because of its ecological, political, social and sexual idiologies and practices. I have stayed there several times and admire and respect ZEGG because members really do live their phylosophy, love flourishes, and mind and spirit, emotion and intellect are equally honoured.

This group began in southern Germany in 1978, following the teachings of radical sociologist Dr Dieter Duhm. In 1983, Duhm and 40 adherents began a dramatic experiment in communal living, believing they could achieve personal growth through practicing 'free-love' and clear and open communication. In 1991, following the collapse of East Germany, they bought 15 hectares (40 acres) of land about an hour south-west of Berlin. This former STASI (Secret Police) training camp had several houses, an apartment block, hotel and study/conference centre. The 80 members re-named it ZEGG, an acronym for 'Zentrum für Experimentelle Gesellschaftsgestaltung', or Centre for Experimental Cultural Design.

Today, ZEGG has 70 adults (one-third of whom are men) and 20 children. Most members are well educated, often with professional training. They range in age from early 20s to 70s, with most in their 30s and 40s. According to ZEGG's website, their common thread is 'the quest for new forms of love, sexuality and the manifestation of inner and outer peace', while establishing 'an international conference and research centre working on draft models for socially and ecologically sustainable ways of living'.

ZEGG is best known for their polyamorous ways. While sometimes called 'free-love', a more accurate phrase is 'love without limits'. Members not only have sex with multiple partners, but aim for 'love free of fear, mistrust and jealousy' because, according to member Ina Meyer-Stoll, 'if you are really free of these, then you will surely go to several lovers'. Jealousy still arises occasionally, but they deal with it through open and honest discussion. Many members are in long-term, stable relationships, although rarely monogamous. Sexual relations between members and guests are common, with precautions taken against pregnancy and sexually transmitted diseases. All forms of sexuality are openly practiced, heterosexual and homosexual, polygamous and monogamous, long-term and short-term. The only form of sexuality which is unacceptable is where exploitation occurs. Some critics, without having stayed at ZEGG, regard them as immoral. Having lived there three times, for up to a month, I regard them as a highly ethical intentional communitiy.

ZEGG has a relatively low birth rate. Some children live with their parents while others live in Children's House, but all are cared for and supported by the community. Several young people live there although their parents have left. ZEGG youth appear to be more conservative than their parents.

Minor decisions are made within work groups such as kitchen, conferences, children's house, garden and maintenance. Community-wide decisions are first discussed within a 'Council of 13'—representing all the working areas. Decisions by this Council become community decisions unless somebody objects, in which event the matter is referred to a meeting of all members where the issue is resolved by consensus.

Members have refined a form of communal meeting called 'The Forum', which they describe as

> *a ritualised and creative form of communication ... a stage upon which each member's thoughts, feelings and anything that moved them can become visible to others. This supports a healthy transparency when it comes to the issues of love or power ... and it helps to maintain a clear distinction between factual discussion and emotional processes.*

Each member is responsible for her/his own income. About half work off-site, or at on-site businesses such as Ökotec, an environmental planning consultancy, a bookshop and mail-order business, an ecological building firm, graphics studio, website layout office, and a business coaching firm. Other members work directly for ZEGG. Everyone pays ZEGG for rent and food, regardless of their income source. ZEGG also earns income from hosting conferences and events, and from businesses which use ZEGG facilities. Members have raised and invested over €3,000,000 (US$3,500,000 or £2,200,000) into their communal property.

A great deal of ZEGG's work, money and creativity goes into environmental projects. They have their own fresh water supply and, at times, sell water to the local council. They treat all human wastes and recycle onto their garden and fruit trees. They grow a great deal of organic food. Their buildings are heated and hot water supplied through an efficient furnace, using woodchips which would otherwise become land-fill. Many of their formerly ugly buildings have been retrofitted with insulation and for passive solar heating and cooling, and painted bright colours.

Members and guests eat almost all their (vegetarian) meals in ZEGG's dining room. They have their own pub, the 'Dorfkneipe', which is a common meeting place. They also have a pottery, cafe, swimming pool, sauna, art-room, library and other facilities whereby members live cultured and contented lives. Members spend a great deal of time together and socialising can be quite intense.

Potential ZEGG members undertake an intensive, two month

Community Training Program, during which their social, sexual and ideological norms are challenged. Many find polyamorous communality too challenging, and leave. The others then do a three month trial membership after which they are eligible to be accepted as full members. Because of ZEGG's financial system, most new members need a job or a small business that they can operate from ZEGG.

Members see themselves 'as an experimental community working together to develop models which serve this vision in the different parts of our lives. As well as political engagement and community-building, our work also includes ecology, love and sexuality, our spiritual search, and living with children.' ZEGG is a good example of 'revolution by lifestyle', because members believe that 'a new basis for love, loving openly and freely, without sexual limitations and jealousy, is a social and cultural revolution'. They believe that open relationships are revolutionary, and offer the rest of society a beacon. My ZEGG friend, Christa Falkenstein, says, 'we see our community experiment as a contribution to a general cultural alternative'.

They have been on this path for many years and have been remarkably successful. While not without problems, ZEGG demonstrates that many serious problems of serial monogamy can be avoided, that people can escape from jealousy and live a healthy, erotic life without exploitation. Intentional communities and individuals around the globe can benefit from ZEGG's wisdom.

✍ Contact: ZEGG, Rosa-Luxemburg-Strasse 89, D-14806, Belzig, GERMANY

Website: http://www.zegg.de/englisch/eng.htm

Further Reading: Bill Metcalf's article, 'ZEGG'.

SUMMARY AND CONCLUSION

These eleven intentional communities, each in its own way, are doing well although each has a range of challenges. Each is 'successful' merely by continuing to exist within a not very supportive environment—yet each of them falls short of its potential.

In Chapter Seven, I discuss various intentional community issues, and frequently refer to the intentional communities just described. In the next chapter, however, I digress to look at how to join an intentional community.

Chapter 6

JOINING/FORMING AN INTENTIONAL COMMUNITY

Having read the previous chapter, readers might want to know how to join one of these intentional communities or something similar, or even wonder about forming their own. This is one of the most common questions which people ask and, like most difficult questions, has both simple and complex answers.

The first step for any would-be intentional community member is to learn about the wide range of groups which exist, and try to get information about and a feel for these. At the same time, the prospective member should examine her/his own motivations, expectations, strengths and weaknesses, willingness and ability to contribute, and social, ethical and cultural boundaries. I shall discuss these points in turn.

LOCATING AND LEARNING ABOUT INTENTIONAL COMMUNITIES

The best initial step to learn about the intentional communities in the area where one wishes to live is to consult one of the intentional community directories. In North America, the best directory is *Communities Directory* which can be accessed either in hard copy or on the web. For UK, the best directory is *Diggers and Dreamers*, updated and published every two years. The best directory to intentional communities throughout Europe is *Eurotopia*, available in German and English. *Eco-villages & Communities in Australia and New Zealand*, and *From Here to Nirvana: The Yoga Journal Guide to Spiritual India*, are just what their titles say. As already explained, all of the above directories, unfortunately, miss many intentional communities in the area which they try to cover but this observation is not to criticise the people who published these. It is a simple fact that many intentional communities do not wish to be included in a directory. For details on the above publications, see the Appendix.

As well as the above mentioned publications, there are several books available which, while not directories as such, provide a great deal of information about intentional communities around the globe. My own book, *Shared Visions, Shared Lives: Communal Living Around the Globe* is, in my humble opinion, the best of these but unfortunately it is out of print although copies are held in many Libraries. That book tells fifteen in-depth, personal stories from intentional communities in Canada, USA, Mexico, Brazil, UK, France, Germany, Israel, India, Japan and New Zealand. Another one of my books, *From Utopian Dreaming to Communal Reality* uses the same technique to tell the story of members from ten intentional communities in Australia. Fortunately, it is still in print. *Ecovillage Living: Restoring the Earth and Her People,* by Hildur Jackson and Karen Svensson, looks at the ecovillage movement and offers insights into this part of the intentional community movement.

Numerous magazines and periodicals are published which can help a person learn about and locate an intentional community. The best of these is *Communities* magazine, published by the Fellowship for Intentional Community. Although it tries to provide international coverage, most of the material is North American. Most other western countries have similar, but less professional, magazines and newsletters. An excellent one with global coverage is CALL (Communes at Large Letter), published in Israel but distributed worldwide.

Several excellent videos can help in identifying the type of intentional community one seeks, and helping to find this. The best is probably Geoph Kozeny's recently released *Visions of Utopia: Experiments in Sustainable*

Culture, Although its coverage is mainly of USA, the examples it shows can be found elsewhere.

There are numerous web sites which can help connect would-be members and intentional communities, as listed in the Appendix.

YOUR MOTIVATIONS, EXPECTATIONS, STRENGTHS/WEAKNESSES, CONTRIBUTIONS AND BOUNDARIES

In my experience, many people look upon an intentional community as being able to solve their social, financial and emotional problems, look after them, and help them to grow and live a sustainable, ethical life. That may well all be true, but at this stage it is more important to examine what the person in question might be able to contribute to an intentional community, and ask if that person's expectations are reasonable and achievable, given her/his limitations and boundaries. After all, intentional communities, like any social group, are little more than the totality of the inputs and interactions of members. In other words, you need to put energy and commitment into an intentional community before you can reasonably expect to reap any rewards.

It is important to examine your boundaries between the personal and the collective: How much are you willing to share? How much private space do you feel that you need? How much control do you want to maintain over your own property and living space? All forms of intentional community living require some compromise of one's personal space and possessions for the common good. Some groups, often known as communes, might require the pooling of all income and assets, sharing the same living space, and eating and spending most time together. At the other end of a spectrum would be land-owning cooperatives where members have their own houses and might only see other members once a month for a meeting. Cohousing tries to strike a happy medium with members having their own private residences but eating and socialising regularly as a group. It is crucial that any would-be member understand her/his personal preferences and limitations in this regard, and tries to match these with an appropriate group.

If you wish to be in an intentional community where you can be sure of being cared for when ill, of being financially supported when unemployed and of being loved and accepted as if in a family, then you need to find a communal group in which you can selflessly invest these same qualities. If you wish to maintain your own money, residence and independence, then it makes no sense to expect the group to take care of you. With intentional communities, as with most aspects of life, you get out roughly what you put in.

VISITING AND JOINING AN INTENTIONAL COMMUNITY

Having located an intentional community which roughly complies with your expectations and abilities, it is important to make contact and arrange to visit. Many large intentional communities have open days and other formal ways to make that first visit very easy, while smaller groups will simply agree on a mutually convenient time for you to come. Never join an intentional community if it is the only one you have visited, and never visit just once. Discuss with various members what you want and can offer, and ensure that you understand the financial and legal arrangements, the social, dietary and sexual norms, any spiritual expectations and, last but not least, any restrictions on pets, visitors, drugs, diet and dress.

As with dating to find one's 'perfect partner', be prepared for many disappointments and setbacks. Accept that the vast majority of intentional communities may not suit you—nor you them. During more that 30 years of research, I have visited several hundred intentional communities but only a handful appeal to me personally as places where I might wish to live for a long time. Do not give up if you find that what you hoped might be utopia is really a social ghetto, and those supposedly leading the ideal life are really idiots and immoral misfits, at least in your eyes. Keep looking and, while re-examining your wants, boundaries and contributions, the perfect intentional community may well find you.

FORMING AN INTENTIONAL COMMUNITY

I strongly advise anyone against trying to form an intentional community, at least until after he/she has accumulated many years of experience in other groups. Learn about your own boundaries, abilities, practical strengths and shortfalls. Learn with what form of governance and economic exchange you are comfortable. Learn what you think of various sorts of spirituality and of rituals. Only then, if you have not found the combination which suits you and, having deeply introspected and thought/meditated upon the question and are convinced that you are not projecting your own shortcomings, and that your desire is achievable—only then do I suggest you consider forming an intentional community.

But, be warned. Most dreamed-of intentional communities never reach the serious planning stage; of those that do, most never even start; of those that start, most collapse within the first two years; and of those survivors, most will collapse within five years. The odds are very much against the long term survival of any intentional community you might form—but that does not mean that you should not do so. After all, the best known and longest lasting intentional communities around the globe, such as Findhorn Foundation, Damanhur, Twin Oaks, Crystal Waters and The Farm were once nothing but fuzzy ideas.

A good article to read prior to visiting your first intentional community is Geoph Kozeny's *Red Carpets and Slammed Doors.* Probably the best book available to help you in forming an intentional community, should you be determined to do so, is Diana Leafe Christian's *Creating a Life Together: Practical Tools to Grow Ecovillages and Intentional Communities.* Although most of the examples are from USA, her observations and principles are universally applicable.

In my next chapter, we look at the issues which are common to all intentional communities, and I shall describe how some groups have resolved them. It will become obvious that there is no 'recipe book' for intentional community—but a host of good lessons which can be learnt and which will greatly increase your chances of successfully living the intentional community lifestyle—whatever that means to you.

Chapter 7

ISSUES OF LIVING IN INTENTIONAL COMMUNITY

This chapter addresses the key issues or problems of intentional community life. Many of these issues are, of course, the very factors that help intentional communities to meet at least some of their members' needs, hopes and dreams. Their resolution is crucial for the group to survive, thrive and become a model for sustainable living.

It is important to remember that in spite of untold years of research by many scholars from around the globe there are few, if any, universally agreed upon maxims or rules for intentional community living. There is no magical recipe which, if followed, will guarantee a successful intentional community—nor indeed even agreement on how to measure success. The best that I can do here is explain the options, and provide rules of thumb, the ways which generally work, at least in my own communal experience, from my own and other scholars' research, and from heeding the wisdom of long-term intentional community members.

Whenever people consider living within an intentional community, it is only too easy for them to imagine a host of potential problems—often more than enough to deter them. Many of these potential problems are challenges to intentional community life but that is all they are—challenges which are solvable rather than insurmountable barriers. There are two main reasons why people anticipate so many problems of living in intentional community.

Firstly, almost everyone who is joining or forming an intentional community comes from a society in which the isolated nuclear family is the norm, and from a culture in which competition is far more important than cooperation, where it is assumed that one must look after oneself first and foremost, and that it is naive to trust people other than immediate family. Ours is a culture in which individualism is commonly understood as suggesting that collective action is likely to be personally inhibiting and against one's own best interests. A vague and naive notion of 'individual freedom' is often relied upon as an excuse to avoid collective action even when such action might benefit everyone.

Secondly, wherever I have worked around the world I have found that the popular media, both electronic and print, generally have negative, patronising images of intentional communities. Conflict is the life-blood of the media, and there is no obvious story in, for instance, a religiously-oriented intentional community which thrives. As soon as things go wrong, however, the media will label it a 'nasty cult', and then there is a story. Occasionally, media stories look at people who were once radical communards, who shared everything, including money and sex, but who today live in, for example, a cohousing group. They suggest that because these people have changed, the original impetus must somehow be wrong and therefore this person and community 'failed'. I know of no-one, including reporters and media commentators, who has not changed. Change is healthy and normal, and does not indicate failure.

That said, I shall briefly discuss a wide range of issues within intentional communities: money, property, governance, conflict resolution, gender relations, sex, children, privacy, drugs, shared visions, rituals, socialisation, old & young, commitment and other issues.

MONEY

Not surprisingly, money is an issue within every intentional community—although probably not such a big issue as within the wider society. In my experience, most conflicts over money within intentional communities arise because of poor communication and unclear rules and norms. These lead some members to feel they are contributing too much or receiving too little, either in total or compared to others. The sources of this conflict include simply not having enough money, and disagreements over the allocation of money and financial responsibility between the individual and the collective.

There are two 'idealised' models of intentional community finance. In one, individual members are responsible for the collective while in the other the collective is responsible for the individual.

In the first model, each member is responsible for her/his own income, property and money but contributes a stipulated amount into the collective purse, just as people owning land in the conventional way pay local government tax. In intentional communities such as Windsong, The Wolery and Community Alternatives, nearly all collective income comes from the regular contributions of members. Individuals are responsible for their own maintenance and communal charges even when too old or too sick to work. Generally, property is private unless specifically collective. This is by far the most common financial model within newly developing ecovillage and cohousing communities.

In the second model, most or all income is earned by the collective, through communal businesses, and these funds are used to support the members. Darvell Bruderhof, Twin Oaks, Kommune Niederkaufungen and residential staff members of Findhorn Foundation exemplify this system. Almost all members work for the collective which then feeds and houses them. Individuals either receive a small personal allowance or simply request/take cash when needed for private needs. If a member cannot work because of ill-health or old age, she/he is still cared for by the collective. Property generally belongs to the collective unless specifically allocated to individuals. Members might not even own the clothes they wear.

Many intentional communities develop hybrid forms of these two financial models. At Damanhur, Lothlorien and ZEGG, for instance, some members work for and earn money from the collective while others work elsewhere but all income belongs to the individual who contributes to the collective for her/his food and accommodation, regardless of from where that income was derived. On the other hand, at Kadarim and Kommune Niederkaufungen, all income goes into the collective regardless of whether the money was earned by collective or private enterprise. At Kadarim, the collective is responsible for major expenses, and about another 40% of the collective income is distributed to members, the individual amounts depending to some extent on a person's earnings.

Some intentional communities reduce their need for money by creating their own currency for internal transactions, while many others use local complementary currency systems such as LETS. Damanhurians created their own currency, the 'Credito', which has greatly increased their prosperity, and ethically anchors their exchange system to 'values linked to the sustainability of the planet, to the respect for Humankind and all living beings, to respect for work and the added value of well thought out products created with care and love'.

PROPERTY

Few countries have legal systems designed to facilitate property holding by communal groups. In Israel, kibbutzim pre-dated the establishment of the nation, so communal property-holding is reasonably well provided for within their legal system. In most other countries, however, intentional communities have to rely on laws which were designed for social groupings such as co-operatives, churches, non-profit organisations and companies. Some western countries have implemented legislation to facilitate cohousing and ecovillages, usually based on laws applying to strata title for high-rise home units. Within these models, individual property rights are generally greater than the rights of the collective, and this can lead to problems.

In intentional communities such as ZEGG, Darvell Bruderhof, Kadarim, Lothlorien, Findhorn Foundation and Community Alternatives, almost all property belongs to the collective so many potential property problems do not exist—but others may arise. Not everyone is happy to not own any 'real' property and at Kadarim, for instance, housing is now being reassigned from the collective to individuals. While this solves one problem it creates others such as what control the collective will have on the transfer by sale or inheritance of this private property. Findhorn Foundation has been privatising its collective resources for some time although it still owns much property. Intentional communities, like most other social groupings, must maintain control over who can be a member, and ensure membership is used for the common good. This is relatively easy while most property is collectivised but becomes more difficult when property is privatised.

In intentional communities such as The Wolery and Windsong, dwellings are virtually owned by individuals who are also joint owners of the remaining, collective property. This model can create a problem with the sale of houses that can only be sold to an approved applicant. An additional problem at The Wolery is that no mortgage is available to a would-be buyer because houses do not have separate titles. This is quite different from people who see themselves as belonging to a collective which owns the whole property. Some intentional communities have failed simply because individuals have transferred their private property to others who are not interested in communal living, and who thereby sap the collective energy.

Damanhur has a hybrid system wherein most real estate is owned by a co-operative in which members hold shares, allotted according to their investments, and these can be reimbursed if a person leaves. They say that this ensures that 'ownership of communal property is not divided and that wealth remains in common, protected for those who have contributed to its acquisition'.

There is no 'best' model for how to deal with property within an intentional community but the rule of thumb is that the more property that is owned collectively, the closer the group will usually be in social, spiritual and cultural ways—although this may not be a causal relationship. This very closeness and interdependence, of course, is what many would-be and current intentional community members fear, which is why we have the dramatic increase in creative hybrid forms such as cohousing. I am not putting a value judgement on how any intentional community holds their property but it is an important issue with far-reaching implications. To naively start off with the unquestioned assumption that private ownership is best, or worst, seriously limits their social, environmental and political potential.

GOVERNANCE

There are many ways by which contemporary intentional communities govern themselves. Some groups have focused or concentrated power, with one person (or a small clique) making decisions for everyone, while other groups have diffused or shared power with everyone taking part in decision-making. Focused-power decision-making can be called either theocratic or charismatic leadership, while diffused-power, with everyone taking part, can employ majority-rule, democratic voting, or consensus decision-making. In some ways, these four are quite different although in practice they often overlap and complement each other. Many intentional communities follow different methods of governance at different stages of their lifespan, and some groups might use aspects of several methods for resolving one major issue. I try to discuss governance in a way that should help readers to understand the principles, practicalities and possibilities for decision-making within intentional communities, but successful intentional communities, in the real world, eventually work out their own models which are rarely as simple as those that I briefly describe.

FOCUSED POWER DECISION MAKING MODELS

Theocracy: Many religiously-oriented intentional communities follow a theocratic form of governance. In this model, while everyone is equal on one level, not everyone is seen to be at the same point in her/his relationship with the Divine. Because members of such intentional communities are, by definition, interested in following the selected religious model it makes perfect sense for members to follow the leadership of those who have made the greatest spiritual progress. The Bruderhof, Hare Krishna communes, and most religious orders follow this theocratic model, generally combining it with a degree of consensus-building.

There are various ways by which 'elders' or leaders are selected within such intentional communities although it is generally through community-wide recognition of the wisdom of a person's religious devotion, character and pronouncements, combined with some sense of spiritual/divine intervention. In practice, strength of personality and affability also generally play a role. There can either be a single leader or a small leadership group.

This is an efficient system of governance until people either lose their faith or for some reason cannot agree on who is more religiously/spiritually advanced. At that point, such groups generally change to democratic voting or charismatic decision-making. Historically, some intentional communities have followed theocratic governance for several generations with no particular problems. Theocratic leaders do not automatically become despots although the risk is always there.

Charismatic Leadership: This applies where an intentional community is led by someone who operates mainly through strength of personality, the ability to lead and inspire without people feeling dominated, and an ability to magnetically attract the affection, respect and perhaps even adoration of other members.

Findhorn Foundation had this model for the first part of its life (via Peter Caddy) as did ZEGG (via Dieter Duhm) and Damanhur (via Oberto Airaudi). All three of these groups have moved away from charismatic leadership, finding a way for ordinary members to govern their own communities. Often this change from charismatic leadership can be painful, and result in the bitter overthrow and rejection of the leader, but in all of the above examples this did not happen and the previous charismatic leaders are still held in high esteem.

Charismatic leadership is very efficient for making decisions because there is no need for time-consuming discussions, voting, etc. It is assumed that the leader is closer to the heart of the community and its ethos than is anyone else, so when she/he makes a decision it is obviously for the good of all. This efficiency is not only because decisions can be made quickly but also because the leader provides the collective spirit or ethos, and then enshrines, embodies and represents this through decisions. While charismatic leadership is, in general, an efficient form of governance when developing an intentional community, it is generally the worst form to help it endure because ordinary members have no chance to develop leadership skills for when their leader dies or leaves.

DIFFUSED POWER DECISION-MAKING MODELS

Majority Vote, Democratic Decision-Making: Kibbutzim such as Kadarim, and most of the large ecovillages around the globe, such as Crystal Waters in Australia and Auroville in India, use forms of voting, often modified to give a vote to each household or membership share rather than to each person, or perhaps setting other than 50% + 1 as the needed support for decisions and rule changes. In some intentional communities, matters are referred to all interested members who discuss and then vote, with different percentages required for different sorts of decisions, and sometimes by people with different sorts of membership. Some other intentional communities, such as Damanhur, Kadarim, Twin Oaks and ZEGG, have forms of what might loosely be called representational democracy wherein members select a subgroup who then make decisions. Such decisions can, in many cases, then be challenged by members and become subject to consensus. At Twin Oaks, a version of this, known as a 'planner/manager system' seems to have worked well for decades.

Democratic voting systems are easy to understand and are capable of making decisions within a reasonable time period, but have the problem that with majority rule, while there are winners, there are also almost always losers. Intentional communities which use voting generally temper this with a degree of consensus-building, to reduce the problem of having losers since it is hard enough to hold any group together without almost deliberately alienating members. I cannot imagine a close-knit commune using simple majority voting any more than I can picture this working within a healthy family.

Consensus Decision-Making: This is the model of governance to which many readers of this book probably assume that all intentional communities aspire. With consensus decision-making, proposals are introduced, discussed, and eventually decided upon by the group but without voting as such. Typically, a proposal will, if necessary, be modified and remodified to meet people's concerns, perhaps deferred, and when it is time to decide, people either consent to the proposal, 'stand aside', or 'block' it. To stand aside means a person does not agree but is willing to let the matter proceed, while blocking means stopping a proposal.

Some naive critics dismiss consensus by assuming that it simply means that each member can vote to veto any decision. This is simply untrue. Any decision-making system where each member has a simple veto vote is a form of majority rule where a 100% vote is needed on every issue. With consensus decision-making, on the other hand, people work diligently toward getting complete agreement on an issue or, failing that, at least to a position where those who are not in favour are willing to allow the others to carry on, and will 'stand aside', or at least not 'block' the proposal. If the group cannot come to this position then the proposal does indeed fail but it is a far more complex matter than one member simply exercising a veto vote.

In practice, consensus decision-making can take up a great deal of collective time in discussing and modifying a proposal to try to meet the concerns of all participants. Generally, however, once a decision is made, the group will rapidly implement it because there will be no foot-dragging by members who might have been losers had they followed a simple voting exercise. The better the group has been trained in consensus decision-making, and the better the members know and trust each other, the faster they can reach consensus. Good consensus decision-making can become fast and efficient.

While consensus decision-making can work in any size of intentional community, provided members share a collective vision and adhere to similar values, from my observations it works best in small groups where members also spend considerable time together in working, eating, rituals and recreation. The more communal the group, the more appropriate is, or at least easier to implement, consensus decision-making.

Training in consensus facilitation is a very useful skill to have within any intentional community, even where other forms of decision-making might be followed. There are people in many countries who specialise in training intentional community members in consensus decision-making and other issues of power and collective governance. It is a worthwhile investment for an intentional community to obtain professional help in this regard—preferably before they reach a crisis. Beatrice Brigg's book, *Introduction to Consensus*, is an excellent guide to consensus decision-making for facilitators and ordinary members of intentional communities.

Many intentional communities which try to follow a consensus decision-making model have a fall-back position of voting, usually with a large majority, also called 'super-majority', required to make a decision when they deem that consensus has failed. Often, when a community changes away from consensus decision-making it can be a sign of deeper problems within the group. At other times it indicates that they were only following what might be called pseudo or false consensus, without really having been trained in or understanding the process, so failure was almost inevitable.

As described in Chapter Five, both Community Alternatives and Windsong Cohousing follow consensus decision-making, with no fall-back position of voting. The potential problem with this is that occasionally a decision might be urgently needed, without time to achieve consensus, particularly where interpersonal issues muddy the waters. Also, probably through poor training in consensus facilitation, people can become exhausted in trying to achieve consensus, particularly where the lack of a decision really becomes the final decision between two options. A number of consensus facilitators argue against having a fall-back, voting option because they say this indicates that members simply have not understood consensus and have failed to be creative enough to reshape the proposal to meet everyone's concerns. From my observations, however, I recommend that intentional communities following consensus decision-making do have a fall-back position which has been consensually agreed to in advance, and is recognised as only to be taken in extreme circumstances.

An intentional community which understands and practices good consensus decision-making can experience many positive side effects. Less vocal, shyer members can feel empowered, and everyone can feel included and reinvigorated. It can raise members' collective awareness and energy levels, clarify their shared vision, and generate 'we-consciousness'. It is, however, not a magic elixir or panacea, and may not always work with every group in every circumstance.

As Diana Christian, in *Creating a Life Together* (p.58), says, 'in a well-trained group with good facilitation, using consensus can elevate the consciousness of a group. It's not just a decision-making technique, but a philosophy of inclusion, drawing out the ideas, insights, and wisdom of everyone's "piece of the truth".'

Summary of Governance: Each form of governance has its proponents and detractors, and what works well within one intentional community may be disastrous elsewhere. There is no correct or best model for decision-making in all intentional communities. The most appropriate model depends on the group's shared visions and goals, the number of members, their personalities and life experiences, the degree of communality in which members wish to live, and their willingness to be trained in consensus facilitation. Over-riding this, however, is the simple fact that the greater the degree of shared vision, general agreement and consensus within any intentional community, the lower will be members' dissatisfaction, dissension and departures.

Another thing that is clear is that regardless of an intentional community's governance, the clearer are their rules and norms, and the clearer the methods to change those rules and norms, the less conflict will develop.

Perhaps surprisingly, the best examples of where clear rules and norms are essential concern what might be seen as small matters such as pets, diet, drugs, personal/collective property, and visitors.

ACCOUNTABILITY

All types of intentional community imply a degree of mutual trust, for which each member can expect to be held personally accountable. In financial matters, within some less communal groups such as Windsong this may be as simple as having the treasurer's books audited. In other, more communal groups, much more may be expected. Full income-sharing groups such as Kommune Niederkaufungen, Kadarim, Twin Oaks and Darvell Bruderhof require far more accountability because far more is at stake. Such groups will often display all income and expense figures, and some groups even hold meetings at which members' productivity and consumption are discussed. I once attended a meeting in such a group when a member requested money to fly overseas to visit his sick mother. What would be a very personal decision for most of us was made by the group after discussing that person's contribution to the collective. He was given the money.

Accountability also applies within intentional communities other than with finances. Members of most intentional communities are expected to be accountable for what they say, for their relationships, for how they treat communal assets and even for how they interact intimately. Many people find this to be one of the less attractive aspects of intentional community life, feeling that their autonomy is impinged upon by the group, and that they are no longer free 'to be themselves'. There is some basis for this concern because accountability does entail the individual showing due respect to the collective—not a popular notion in our pathologically individualistic society. The catch is that it is individuals respecting the collective needs (and vice versa) that is essential to making intentional community life worth living.

CONFLICT RESOLUTION

Conflict occurs in all social groups, including intentional communities. 'Successful' groups, however defined, tend to have clear communication and decision-making mechanisms in order to avoid most conflict, plus mechanisms for dealing with conflict which nevertheless arises. These latter mechanisms include prayer in religious groups such as Darvell Bruderhof, meditation for groups such as Findhorn Foundation and Lothlorien, open discussion at ZEGG, and occasional mediation for groups such as The Wolery and Twin Oaks. Damanhurians use a structured exercise called the Game of Life, 'a collective experience of transformation of the self and the world, based on fun, challenge and innovation, in order to find that pinch of divine humour in every situation'. Where an intentional community has a charismatic or theocratic leader it is usually that person's job to help resolve conflicts.

In small and more intense intentional communities such as Kommune Niederkaufungen, Lothlorien and ZEGG, conflicts must be resolved for the group to continue. There is just too much stress in living closely with others to allow people to harbour unresolved conflict. This is not the case, however, in some large and dispersed intentional communities where people can carry on for years by more or less ignoring those with whom they are in conflict. This is occasionally found within large ecovillages where people have their own homes and may share very little other than some common property. Even here, however, unresolved conflict is a drag on the social system.

Unresolved conflict is probably the main reason for the break up of intentional communities. Of course one could argue that the reasons for the conflict and for its non-resolution suggest far deeper problems. Unresolved conflict indicates that people have different opinions and strong emotional attachment to those opinions, and that they lack the insight and process skills to enable them to constructively move through the conflict. In *Creating a Life Together* (p. 201), Diana Christian writes,

> *'For life in community to be better than it was before, we've got to be better than we were before. In fact, we need good process skills more when we're involved in community, since the community process tends to trigger faster-than-normal spiritual and emotional growth. The "crucible of community" tends to magnify and reflect back on us our most destructive or alienating attitudes and behaviors.'*

GENDER RELATIONS

Most contemporary intentional communities aspire to gender equality and, compared to the wider society, most are fairly successful in this regard. I have stayed in groups where most of the cooking and home-care was done by women—but then in others it is mostly done by men. Some intentional communities, including most men-only and women-only groups, do not seek gender equality although most would accept equal rights for everyone. I have visited an eco-feminist group where men were seen as inferior, indeed as the root cause of social problems. I have also stayed in a gay men's group where women were allowed in only in exceptional circumstances.

It is important to remember, however, that because men and women may be seen as different within a group's ideology, we cannot simply assume that this translates into inequality. Remember how at Darvell Bruderhof, Justin Peters wrote, 'we feel that women's and men's intrinsic qualities are neither identical nor interchangeable but that they are equal in value. There are precious qualities which are only to be found in women, and precious qualities which are only to be found in men.' Obviously it is reasonable to hold this view without it being assumed to be sexist.

Most intentional communities challenge, in one way or another, gender-specific roles but more often than not the reality is fairly conventional. It is, of course, far easier to be both a mother and a professional worker while living in places such as Kommune Niederkaufungen, Twin Oaks and Damanhur because the collective assumes some financial and parental role. Within most intentional communities, however, we find traditional gender roles being followed by women and men. I am not suggesting that the intentional community movement has failed in this regard—only that far less has been achieved than had been hoped for.

SEX

People who approach an intentional community with voyeuristic hopes are generally disappointed. While it is true that there used to be a reasonable amount of sexual experimentation and demonstration within communal groups, this is now rare. Even ZEGG, the best-known intentional community with overt sexual experimentation goals, finds most members in long-term relationships, albeit often with several people. Intentional communities, with some exceptions, are remarkably conventional in sexual matters and sometimes can be much more moralistic than the wider society.

Sexual exploitation, including rape and child abuse, occasionally occurs in intentional communities but far less often than in the wider community. This is because within an intentional community there are always people around to observe behaviour. The serious sexual exploitation which can continue for years within an isolated nuclear family would soon become common knowledge in an intentional community—and members would put a stop to it. The exception to this is in the rare community where a charismatic, exploitative leader has people so under her/his control that exploitation is not only tolerated but can become the norm. These activities, which we might see as exploitative, however, may be seen by members as part of God's plan or some such thing. This is really quite rare but when it comes to the attention of the media, all intentional communities are tarred with the same brush. This problem is discussed in the next chapter.

There are intentional communities which are exclusively gay or lesbian, while some other communities ban such liaisons and still others which insist on celibacy. Some communities see a member's sexuality to be of collective importance while others see it as a personal matter. In general, our western obsession with serially monogamous heterosexuality as the norm for sexual relationships and rearing of children, who must then remain asexual until well past the age-of-consent, is not challenged but is supported by most intentional communities. While intentional communities may challenge other social norms, with a few exceptions, they are quite conventional on the sexual front.

CHILDREN

With the exception of some religiously-based communities such as Darvell Bruderhof, most intentional communities have relatively low birth rates. While in general it is easier to rear children within a communal environment, people living there often feel less need to do so. This is because most adults enjoy having some interaction with children but in mainstream society this can often be achieved only by having one's own children. The cost of rearing children within the nuclear family can be crippling, and yet the child still has only two adults, and perhaps several siblings, with whom to relate. Within intentional communities, on the other hand, people can relate to children almost as much or as little as they wish without needing to be a parent.

Arguably, children benefit more from living in intentional community than do adults. They quickly develop the ability to relate to other children and to adults other than their kin, and can observe and learn from a wide range of 'teachers'. Both parents and children have little fear of 'stranger danger' because they feel safe within the community. It is common to find the children moving around together, calling in at this or that house to play, eat, or watch what someone is doing, then move on. Parents might not see their children all day yet know that they are safe and that wherever they are, someone will look after them. At The Farm, in USA, this is called 'the kid herd'.

PRIVACY AND AUTONOMY

Privacy is something which most westerners covet although it is an almost unknown concept in many traditional cultures where people feel sorry for anyone who is alone. In intentional communities such as Kommune Niederkaufungen, Twin Oaks, Community Alternatives, Darvell Bruderhof, ZEGG, Damanhur and residential staff members at Findhorn Foundation's Cluny Hill College, where members eat together and live in close proximity, often within the same building, it can be very difficult to maintain private space. An extreme form of this is that at ZEGG where, during their first three months potential members even sleep together with 10-20 others in one large room, without partitions. I once stayed at an intentional community where members showered together and there were not even doors on the toilets!

To help cope with this lack of privacy, many intentional communities such as Findhorn Foundation have a quiet space for prayer/meditation/introspection. Windsong, Kadarim, Lothlorien and the Wolery have members living within self-sufficient housing units, thereby enabling people to regulate time spent alone vs. together. At Twin Oaks and Damanhur members have private rooms, while at Darvell Bruderhof families have private apartments.

The provision of considerable private space is one of the main advantages of cohousing, although it works against them developing a high degree of communality. Not surprisingly, there is a loose, inverse relationship between the degree of communalism and privacy. For hopefully self-evident reasons, intentional communities where the collective is responsible for the individual usually offer less privacy. Where members are responsible for the collective, there is less need to be so intimately involved with each other. It is not unknown within some of the latter communities for people to feel lonely while still within a notional 'communal' group.

Often people who ask me about intentional community living express the fear that should they join they would lose their individual freedom and individuality. It is, of course, true that there is another loose inverse relationship between the degree of communalism and the amount of individual autonomy—but the same applies when one enters a relationship with a sexual partner, for example. Hopefully in both cases the small loss of autonomy is more than offset by the satisfaction of being part of something bigger. It is important to recognise that many people find that they gain personal autonomy in other ways within an intentional community. To know that this group will support you in times of crisis, that you will be cared for when unwell, and accepted for who you are can be a great boost to anyone's sense of personal security and autonomy. But, of course, there is a cost in that one must reciprocate. When this reciprocity threatens to break down, as has happened over the last 20 years in many kibbutzim, people can feel vulnerable.

To live in intentional community, one must be prepared to give up a certain amount of privacy, individuality and autonomy, and believe that this will be more than compensated for by the collective experience.

RECREATIONAL DRUGS

The use of recreational drugs is widespread within western society, and few intentional communities are an exception. Alcohol and caffeine are by far the most common recreational drugs of choice, closely followed by nicotine. Some intentional communities, such as ZEGG, use alcohol regularly as a social lubricant, while most allow alcohol only in moderation, but others, such as Darvell Bruderhof, restrict alcohol to special events such as weddings, and then generally only for men. A few intentional communities ban all stimulants including nicotine, tea and coffee.

'Hard' recreational drugs such as heroin and cocaine occasionally find their way into intentional communities but I know of none where they are tolerated. Marijuana is accepted within some intentional communities although banned in many others. In general, marijuana is probably found less often in intentional communities today compared to when I began my research 30 years back. At that time, marijuana was often used as a sort of sacrament, a ritual to help bind the group and promote collective consciousness. This is now rare although it can still be found.

The old image of stoned communards is largely a relic of media fantasy. When visiting an intentional community one is far more likely to be offered a coffee or herbal tea than a joint.

SHARED VISION

It is certainly not essential for members of an intentional community to agree on every matter—in fact a degree of difference is a positive attribute in promoting flexibility and longevity. But what is important to maintaining a collective group is the holding of some sort of shared vision. The stronger this is held, and the clearer that vision, the more communal the group can become. Some groups have visions that are as simple as 'environmental sustainability' or 'spirituality and equality' which can mean almost anything to anyone. Others, such as ZEGG, Damanhur, Darvell Bruderhof, Kommune Niederkaufungen, Findhorn Foundation and Lothlorien have clear visions of themselves as being able to change society through setting an example. Some of these visions have been collectively devised while for others the vision is religiously or spiritually inspired.

To have no shared vision within an intentional community suggests that communal relationships are based on expediency. This can be sufficient to allow a group with low levels of communality, as might be found in some large land-sharing cooperatives, to continue. Even there, however, it is important that people at least share the vision of making their group a success. When social groups lose all sense of shared vision, interrelationships will deteriorate and become more fragile, and they will break up or simply dissolve and melt away.

RITUALS

Most intentional communities, like almost all other social groupings, have rituals which help members to interconnect more closely. Most of these rituals also have other, more obvious, purposes. Shared meals are the most obvious example of this. For example, during noon meals at Darvell Bruderhof, one member is delegated to read letters from members who are away, make announcements, etc, so that both the meal and the 'entertainment' combine to help create 'we-consciousness', a sense of shared identity. At Findhorn Foundation, their regular Friday night dinners, Saturday 'home-care', KP (Kitchen Patrol) work, and occasional social events, all help unite members. ZEGG's Forum is not only an efficient means of solving problems but also serves as a ritualised binding mechanism. Many intentional communities such as The Wolery, Darvell Bruderhof, Kommune Niederkaufungen, Twin Oaks and Lothlorien use shared work as a ritual, while others use singing and dancing. Damanhur has many rituals including celebrating solstices and equinoxes, and taking part in their Game of Life. It makes little difference what is the form of a ritual but the more communal the group, the more important are rituals, and vice versa.

Community Alternatives seems to have less ritual life now than when I first visited, and the group is less communal. Cohousing groups such as Windsong do not aim for a great deal of communality, so need less ritual, although even there rituals develop. Very intimate groups such as ZEGG, Darvell Bruderhof, Twin Oaks and Kommune Niederkaufungen require far more ritual to bind them together and to maintain high levels of trust. As kibbutzim such as Kadarim privatise their property and economy, I predict that rituals will become less central, although will remain important. A Kadarim member, Gary Favel, disagrees, telling me, 'I think the more we privatise, rituals like Friday night dinners and celebration of festivals such as Shavout and Pesach will take on added importance'. Time will tell.

SOCIALISATION

All social groups require a degree of socialisation for new members, to convert people from 'one-of-them' to 'one-of-us'. Even clubs and sporting teams often have some unique behavioural patterns and cultural norms which must be mastered by a newcomer before she/he is considered to be a full member. We are all familiar with having to learn new behaviours when joining a different school, workplace, social venue or in-law network, and the same applies when joining an intentional community.

Some socialisation occurs even before one joins an intentional community through reading about and perhaps watching videos about the group, as well as through visiting and talking with current members. Once a person joins, the pace of socialisation increases. At large intentional communities such as Findhorn, ZEGG, Damanhur and Darvell Bruderhof, formal courses or programs help acquaint the new member with numerous collective rules and norms, as well as the group's history, mythology and shared culture. In smaller and/or less formal intentional communities socialisation takes place mostly through endless conversations as well as by observing the behaviour of others.

However it occurs, it is important that new members modify their behaviour and world view to fit in with that held by the collective. In looser groups such as many cohousing and ecovillage communities, where most property is privately owned and only limited interaction is expected, this cultural convergence need not be very much. In more intensive groups, where more property is collectively owned and where members interact far more intimately because of living, sleeping, working and dining conditions, the social and cultural convergence needs to be far greater. New members who are not sufficiently socialised will find it difficult to be in the group and may well be a thorn in the side of fellow members. For the long-term survival of the community, it is preferable to help such a person to either adapt or move on.

Socialisation should not be thought of as 'brainwashing', but as a natural process which goes on within all social groups and within all of us during our entire lives. For any collection of people to deserve the title of being an 'intentional community' there must be a degree of shared culture and this can only be achieved through socialisation.

OLD & YOUNG

There is a saying among kibbutzniks that communal living is heaven for young people and seniors but hell for those in between. This is because within any commune such as a kibbutz, as well as at Darvell Bruderhof, Damanhur, Kommune Niederkaufungen and Twin Oaks, children and older people are partially cared for by the collective, and reap the benefits of living within a secure social system even though they are not financially productive. The rest of the members, of course, work and earn the money which supports not just themselves but also those who cannot work. As long as the intentional community lasts, members know that when they get too old to work, they can expect to be supported by the collective. Of course, should the intentional community collapse or radically change its economic system, then by the time these middle aged members reach old age they may find that they have to be self-supporting. This is a problem which some kibbutzniks face as their kibbutzim face financial crises and privatisation.

In general, young and old members are favoured within intentional communities where a great deal of property is collectively owned and where the community collectively earns money and is responsible for members. On the other hand, middle aged people will be favoured within intentional communities where most property is privately owned and where people are responsible for the community. As with all heuristic models, however, intentional communities try to modify their systems to combine the best of all worlds.

COMMITMENT

Commitment is rather out of vogue in modern society, but is essential to the continuation of every healthy social group, be it a family, club, friendship group or intentional community. Unless people are committed to something, they tend to drift from one shallow interest to another, always consuming culture and social capital without contributing. Unfortunately, some people with this lack of depth find their way into intentional communities and are generally a drag on the group, but fortunately, rarely stay long.

Over 30 years ago, an American scholar, Dr Rosabeth Kanter, wrote a seminal book called *Commitment and Community*. In it she looked at commitment mechanisms within historical American communes and concluded that there are three mechanisms by which communal groups promote and ensure the commitment of their members: 'instrumental' commitment, in which the benefits of staying in the group are rationally seen to outweigh the costs; 'affective' commitment, being an attachment to relationships and group solidarity; and 'moral' commitment, based on a sense of what is ethical.

Kanter argued that instrumental commitment depends both on rewards from belonging and on the costs of leaving, which she called 'sacrifice' and 'investment'. Instrumental commitment is promoted if members give up, or sacrifice, something in order to join, and then invest all their time, energy and resources into the group without any hope of recouping this should they leave.

Affective commitment, she asserted, is promoted through 'renunciation' and 'communion'. Renunciation involves giving up relationships outside the group (as, for example, a nun forsaking her family). Communion results from members having wide-ranging and meaningful contact with most members of the group, and developing a 'we-consciousness'.

Moral commitment, Kanter believed, is based on 'mortification' and 'transcendence'. Mortification results from suppressing one's individual identity for one which is shaped by the community. Transcendence involves an individual in surrendering her/his self-will to the collective will of the group. Through mortification, people lose their extreme individualism, while transcendence helps people find themselves once again within a greater collectivity.

Although these commitment-generating mechanisms no doubt sound rather drastic for readers wondering about joining an ecovillage or cohousing project, they can operate anywhere, although on a more limited scale. The most obvious place where people develop strong commitment is within sexual relationships and families, where the above mechanisms can be easily seen.

Within intentional communities, high levels of commitment are most obvious within religious and spiritual groups although all groups require some commitment to survive. Because many contemporary people seem to be 'commitment-shy', it can be difficult for them to live within an intentional community because they cannot manage even the low level of commitment needed in a land-sharing co-operative. They may well crave for the closeness which only a deep level of commitment would enable while perversely being unable to contribute to this.

As a rule of thumb, the more deeply members are committed to their intentional community, the more meaningful, healthy and supportive the group becomes. Of course I could just as easily have phrased this the other way round: the more meaningful, healthy and supportive an intentional community becomes, the more deeply will members commit to it. Worthwhile intentional communities need committed members—and committed members develop worthwhile intentional communities!

OTHER ISSUES

It is important to remember that when people join an intentional community they bring along their emotional 'baggage', so the petty problems which crop up for all of us in our workplace, neighbourhood and family can also crop up within community. Intentional communities rarely avoid issues such as envy, jealousy, selfishness, attachment and malice, but they can often provide a safe environment and the mechanisms to deal effectively with these problems. Intentional communities which last for a long time always have mechanisms to resolve the many small issues with which we humans annoy and pester each other. These mechanisms include meditation at Findhorn and Lothlorien, prayer at Darvell Bruderhof, the Game of Life at Damanhur, and the Forum at ZEGG.

CONCLUSION

People in intentional communities do not have a stress-free lifestyle but they at least have the mechanisms to help deal with the stresses of modern social life. When joining any intentional community, one can expect some new issues to be raised, and to find oneself challenged in various ways, but all successful communities help members to deal with these. In general, people within intentional communities have less stressful and more committed and satisfying lives compared to their previous experience, and to the general population.

Chapter 8

INTENTIONAL COMMUNITIES AS CULTS?

No book about intentional communities should ignore the popular media perception that at least some of them are 'wicked cults'. I say this not because many intentional communities are cults, however that word might be defined, but because this is a serious issue through which many worthwhile intentional communities have been and are being damaged by the frenzied hysteria of so-called 'cult-busters'.

There have always been a few intentional communities which, at least to the outsider, appear to exploit members, and some are occasionally downright dangerous. The five best known, recent examples of this are: 1) Jonestown, in northern Guyana, where 918 people, including their leader, Reverend Jim Jones, died by murder and suicide on November 18, 1978; 2) the Branch Davidian Adventists, Texas, where 74 people, including their leader, David Koresh (Vernon Howell) died in a fire on April 19, 1993; 3) the Solar Temple, France, Switzerland and Canada, led by Luc Jouret, of which 53 people died by poisoning, shooting and fire on October 4-5, 1994, with another 16 deaths on December 22, 1995, and a further 5 deaths on March 22, 1997; 4) Aum Shinrikyo (Aum Supreme Truth Religion) Japan, led by Asahara Shoko, which launched sarin nerve gas attacks on Tokyo subway lines on March 20, 1995, killing 12 people and injuring over 5000 others; and 5) Heaven's Gate, USA, led by Marshall Applewaite, with 39 members murdering each other or committing suicide on or about March 22, 1997. A detailed coverage of these tragic groups is provided by John Hall in *Apocalypse Observed.*

Less deadly but equally well-known groups which have frequently been accused of being cults include the Unification Church, the Children of God (renamed The Family), the International Society for Krishna Consciousness (known as Hare Krishnas), the Divine Light Mission, the Church Universal and Triumphant, and the Church of Scientology. Not all of these religious groups form intentional communities, although most have some members living communally.

The above mentioned intentional communities and groups, and their actions, have at various times become popular media stories and have resulted in many other intentional communities, with no connection to them, also being accused of being wicked cults. In Japan, for example, the Yamagishi communes, which are often likened to kibbutzim, were almost driven into bankruptcy by the anti-cult hysteria sparked by the Aum Shinrikyo incident of 1995. Those tragic events, without connection to Yamagishi, led to an anti-intentional community backlash.

Anti-cult hysteria is not a new phenomenon. From my research into Herrnhut, Australia's first intentional community, almost as soon as it started in 1852 critics began accusing it of all sorts of nasty, cult-like behaviour such as sexually abusing children and sharing sexual partners. Extensive research showed firstly that criticism came mainly from those who knew the least about the commune, and secondly I found almost no research support for these allegations. The early Mormons, and Oneida, in USA, had to move home several times because of violent persecution over their allegedly cultish behaviour. The Children of God (aka Shakers) in 19th century England, and Federative Home in 19th century New Zealand were likewise persecuted with a host of anti-cult sentiments—almost always untrue. The use of pejorative terms to promote political ends is a common practice across time and cultures. It continues today with the all too frequent accusation that any intentional community with which some people do not see eye-to-eye must be a cult.

This litany of anti-intentional community hysteria indicates that it is a common response from people who are confronted with social alternatives, no matter how benign they might be. Of course, to some greedy and would-be oppressive people any social alternative is a threat. Frankly, any intentional community which does not provoke some opposition is probably unlikely to be radical enough to achieve much anyhow. To be accused by some ill-informed and bigoted critics of being cult-like might just indicate that the intentional community is achieving something!

As Professor Melton points out in *The Encyclopedia of Community* (p. 359),

> *The choice to adopt a belief and practice that separates a group from the larger community often makes the group the target of criticism and discrimination. This problem becomes most acute when group life undermines commonly accepted social conventions that value family ties, individual accountability, participation in national life, and economic productivity.*

Anyhow, what is a cult? My Macquarie Dictionary defines a cult as:

> *1. a particular system of religious worship, especially with reference to its rites and ceremonies.*
>
> *2. an instance of an almost religious veneration for a person or thing, especially as manifested by a body of admirers.*
>
> *3. the object of such devotion.*
>
> *4. a popular fashion; fad.*

According to the first three parts, devout Roman Catholics and the Pope should fit in, as would some Buddhists and the Dalai Lama, as well as some members of the Republican Party and President George W Bush in USA! There is no reason to assume that such devotion is inherently bad, in fact it is quite normal.

The best tongue-in-cheek definition I have seen for 'cult' was in a cartoon which said something like 'cult members are those people who belong to the church just down the road from mine'!

During my years of research into intentional communities, I have never been with a group to which I would attach the label of cult. I have certainly been in communities where exploitation occurs, although only some of these had charismatic leaders. But then I have seen similar exploitation in many 'normal' families. In any event, whether or not someone is being exploited must be determined in their eyes, not mine. Some intentional communities appear to me to have unhealthy relationships, and it can be difficult for some people to leave exploitative relationships in a community, just as in a family. In some communities I have felt uncomfortable with what was going on—but the same can apply when I visit some families. I have been in a couple of intentional communities where it later came to light that children were being sexually abused but I would not call these 'cults' since such abuse can occur in all sorts of relationships. In fact such abuse is far less likely to occur in an intentional community than in a nuclear family.

There is no tendency for intentional communities, even those with strong charismatic leaders, to become abusive and cult-like, although it occasionally happens. Four mechanisms help intentional communities remain healthy and devoid of cult-like qualities: humour, flexible leadership, movement of people in and out, and education about community. I will now briefly explore these.

It is important for intentional communities to be able to occasionally laugh at themselves, to see the humour and occasional silliness in what they do. I remember my first time at Findhorn Foundation, in 1982, when, in a community cabaret show, members had a skit which poked fun at their founders, while another skit made fun of their own spiritual practices. People who can occasionally laugh at themselves will usually retain their sanity.

Over time, if most members feel that they have some leadership or decision-making role, regardless of how small, the group will not err. Even with a charismatic leader, other members ought to feel that they are responsible for certain areas or aspects of communal life. This not only helps the group to survive if the leader suddenly disappears, but also helps avoid possible exploitation by that leader. It also makes it easier to depose a charismatic leader, if necessary.

It is healthy for an intentional community to occasionally have some members leaving and others joining because this brings in new ideas while helping to resolve otherwise irresolvable personality disputes. It also means that there is some sort of on-going check on what is happening in the group, and increases the likelihood that any abuse will become public knowledge.

Intentional communities which promote education about this social movement are less likely to get into trouble because members can see how things operate elsewhere, what problems others have encountered, and how others have resolved their problems. I worry whenever I encounter intentional community members who think that their way is the ONLY way, because it is all too easy for them to be duped. Intentional communities, to remain healthy, should be interested in what is being done by other intentional communities.

In conclusion, my research and involvement with intentional communities does not lead me to naively think that they are all socially and morally uplifting. Far from it! Some intentional communities are exploitative and a few are dangerous, at least to the emotional well-being of members. The malicious labelling of such groups as 'cults', however, has far more to do with political expediency than with rational analysis or humanitarian concerns. Even the most benign intentional community can become exploitative—just as the nicest person can become a serial killer. The fear of intentional communities turning into wicked cults is grossly over-rated. In almost all intentional communities, individuals are far safer from exploitation than they would have been in the wider society.

Chapter 9

CONCLUSION AND FUTURE OF INTENTIONAL COMMUNITIES

I have devoted most of my adult life to studying intentional communities, and from this work, I offer three macro observations. Firstly, there clearly appears to be some innate human drive toward living in community, and for many creative and passionate people throughout recorded history, this has resulted in them creating or joining an intentional community in order to live a better or perhaps even an ideal life. Secondly, this intentional community movement is growing dramatically in terms of the number of people who are involved and in the countries where such social experiments are found. Thirdly, different styles of intentional community come in and out of favour, but almost all specific groups follow a pattern of becoming less communal and more individualistic over time.

The three main areas of demographic growth within the intentional community movement are ecovillages, cohousing and new religious groups.

Ecovillages are becoming so popular throughout much of the world that many people imagine them to be the only type of intentional community. Most ecovillages are located in rural or semi-rural areas, and have a secular, environmental ethic with relatively low levels of communalism. In some ecovillages, people develop close social and economic affiliations and live close-knit, almost communal lives, but in others little more than common ownership of collective land binds people together. The main attraction of the ecovillage model seems to be that people can live in attractive, rural or semi-rural environments, within a pleasant neighbourhood of like-minded people, while maintaining one's financial, cultural and social independence.

Around the globe, ecovillages are achieving a great deal, promoting environmental education, ecological design and building. They are a non-threatening model for how ordinary people can escape the pressures of contemporary cities, and live closer to nature and to each other. The ecovillage movement will continue to develop both with the growth of existing groups and development of new ones. In some countries, even regional planners and local governments now promote ecovillages.

The cohousing movement is similar to the ecovillage movement in many ways, although most cohousing groups are in urban or suburban areas, and an environmental ethic is sometimes less obvious, although still present, being replaced to some extent by a social ethic. Cohousing members maintain their own money, and some even live with relatively little interaction with other members, although that is rare. They can usually sell their private space on the open market. As with ecovillages, some members may have a minimal commitment to the collective. Many cohousing groups develop high levels of communal interaction and commitment, but individualism is generally favoured over collective needs. An advantage of cohousing is that members can generally maintain their city employment and social networks, while living in a more socially cohesive and supportive group. The research of Dr Graham Meltzer, and others, shows that cohousing is an environmentally-friendly option, with lower consumption of power and other resources compared to members' pre-cohousing lifestyles. The cohousing movement is developing rapidly, particularly in western Europe, North America, Australia and New Zealand.

One could argue that ecovillages and cohousing groups could achieve more in terms of living lightly on the earth if they were more communal—but then one could counter with the argument that these groups may only exist because they are not intensely communal. Perhaps it is environmentally better to have a large number of people taking part in modestly communal cohousing and ecovillages rather than only a few people living in communes and sharing everything? Many people today would not live in intentional community if they had to surrender more individualism.

For quite different reasons from those promoting ecovillages and cohousing, an increasing number of people are being attracted to religiously-based communal groups. The breakdown of traditional family values, the mobility of community-less people, and the common human urge to belong to something both certain and greater than oneself, probably accounts for this popularity. It can be very attractive to many people to escape from moral relativism and uncertainty, from an anomic life where they seem to be mere cogs in a wheel, and to join a group where the rules are clear, the roles are prescribed, and they know they are part of a cohesive group, all walking together on a spiritual path.

Another possible explanation for the extraordinary popularity of some of these new religious communes may simply be because people do indeed receive a divine calling, and it is possible that some groups have been chosen by God, however defined, and really are on the path to salvation. As a scholar, I have problems with this sort of explanation but admit to its possibility.

New religious intentional communities have generally been founded either by charismatic members of traditional religions, or by isolated mystics who believe that through revelation they have discovered a new religious base. Many of the latter, of course, still demonstrate overtones based on their cultural history.

Most religiously-oriented intentional communities are supportive of members, and collectively do a great deal of social good. Some of them also have high environmental ethics and standards. On the other hand, a few of these groups appear to outsiders to abuse their members, although this is rarely the opinion of those who are supposedly being abused. While ecovillages and cohousing groups are almost always tolerant and supportive of other forms of intentional communities, many religious groups are not. Some refuse to be associated with the intentional community movement, preferring to see themselves as the one and only model for intentional community life. These groups worry me.

Evidence suggests that religious intentional communities, based on revealed wisdom, will continue to increase and prosper. It can be environmentally efficient to live as a close-knit commune and it is wonderful to feel surrounded by loving, fellow communards, all bound for salvation following the revealed religious truth.

There is no evidence that other main forms of intentional community, such as secular urban communes, will come back into favour—but who knows.

I have described intentional communities which can be seen as part of an old-fashioned tradition, and setting the agenda for the 21st century, and have pointed out the cyclical nature of these experiments. It may well be that the intensely intimate model of sexual openness as found at ZEGG will become popular and spawn new groups, or it might simply disappear. The all-inclusive collective economy at Kommune Niederkaufungen and Twin Oaks might swing back into popular favour, and groups such as Findhorn Foundation and Kadarim might revert from privatisation to collectivisation. I see no evidence of such trends developing, but equally I have no doubt that they could do so.

The only certainty about intentional communities is that while it is certain that people will continue to develop and live in them, there is very little certainty about which forms they will take.

Finally:

Having read about intentional communities, you might wish to go further. I attach an Appendix with items for further reading, and directories and web sites which you can use to progress along the path to living more communally.

If you are interested in intentional community living, learn what sorts of intentional communities are in your area, make contact and arrange to visit. Intentional community living is experiential, meaning that one of the best ways to learn is to jump in and see how it feels.

To all of you would-be intentional community people, as well as all those people already living in such communities around the globe, I entend all my best wishes for the future and for your efforts to create a more humane and sustainable world.

Appendix

Books and Articles Cited, and Suggested Further Reading

Bang, J. & Bakker, P. (2003) 'Intentional Communities in Scandinavia and the Low Countries', in K. Christensen and D. Levinson, (eds), Encyclopedia of Community: From the Village to the Virtual World. Thousand Oaks, USA: Sage, pp. 748-52.
Bogliolo, K. & Newfeld, C. (2003) In Search of the Magic of Findhorn. Findhorn, UK: Findhorn Press.
Borio, L. (2003) 'Intentional Communities in Italy, Spain, Portugal', in K. Christensen and D. Levinson, (eds), Encyclopedia of Community: From the Village to the Virtual World. Thousand Oaks, USA: Sage, pp. 736-8.
Borstelmann, S. (1997) 'Kommune Niederkaufungen', in Communities, # 94, pp. 52-5.
Briggs, B. (2000) Introduction to Consensus. Cuernavaca, Mexico: Beatrice Briggs. (available in English and Spanish at: http://www.iifac.org)
Brumann, C. (2003) 'Intentional Communities in Japan', in K. Christensen and D. Levinson, (eds), Encyclopedia of Community: From the Village to the Virtual World. Thousand Oaks, USA: Sage, pp. 739-43.
Bulman, J. (1996) 'Love-Puddlers and Social Activists', in W. Metcalf (ed.), Shared Visions, Shared Lives: Communal Living Around the Globe. Findhorn, UK: Findhorn Press, pp. 40-51.
Christian, D. (2003) Creating a Life Together: Practical Tools to Grow Ecovillages and Intentional Communities. Gabriola Island, Canada: New Society Publishers.
Christian, D. (2003) 'Intentional Communities and Governance', in K. Christensen and D. Levinson, (eds), Encyclopedia of Community: From the Village to the Virtual World. Thousand Oaks, USA: Sage, pp. 693-7.
Christophe, S. (1996) 'A Brazilian Community in Crisis', in W. Metcalf (ed) Shared Visions, Shared Lives: Communal Living Around the Globe. Findhorn, UK: Findhorn Press, pp. 166-75.
Clayes, G. (2000) 'Socialism and Utopia', in R. Schaer, G. Clayes and L. Sargent (eds) Utopia-The Search for the Ideal Society in the Western World. New York: Oxford University Press, pp. 206-41.
Coates, C. (2001) Utopia Britannica: British Utopian Experiments 1325-1945. London, UK: Diggers and Dreamers.
Coates, C. (2003) 'Intentional Communities in the United Kingdom and Ireland', in K. Christensen and D. Levinson, (eds), Encyclopedia of Community: From the Village to the Virtual World. Thousand Oaks, USA: Sage, pp. 752-8.
Conochie, E. (1995) 'From Communism to Communalism', in B. Metcalf (Ed.) From Utopian Dreaming to Communal Reality, Sydney, Australia: University of New South Wales Press, pp 171-85.
Corbett, J. & Corbett, M. (2000) Designing Sustainable Communities: Learning From Village Homes. Washington, USA: Island Press.
Durnbaugh, D. (2003) 'Bruderhof', in K. Christensen and D. Levinson, (eds), Encyclopedia of Community: From the Village to the Virtual World. Thousand Oaks, USA: Sage, pp. 101-5.
Eggers, U. (1988) Community for Life. Scottdale, USA: Herald Press.
Ferguson, J. (1975) Utopias of the Classical World. London, UK: Thames and Hudson.
Fogarty, R. (1980) Dictionary of American Communal and Utopian History. Westport, USA: Greenwood Publishing Group.
Fogarty, R. (1990) All Things New: American Communes and Utopian Movements, 1860-1914.

Chicago, USA: University of Chicago Press.
Forster, P. & Metcalf, W. (2000) 'Communal Groups: Social Laboratories or Places of Exile?', in Communal Societies, vol. 20, pp. 1-11.
Gavron, D. (2000) The Kibbutz: Awakening From Utopia. Lanham, USA: Rowman & Littlefield.
Gavron, D. (2003) 'Intentional Communities in Israel—Current Movement', in K. Christensen and D. Levinson, (eds), Encyclopedia of Community: From the Village to the Virtual World. Thousand Oaks, USA: Sage, pp. 727-30.
Gering, R. (2003) 'Intentional Communities in Eastern Europe and Russia' in K. Christensen and D. Levinson, (eds), Encyclopedia of Community: From the Village to the Virtual World. Thousand Oaks, USA: Sage, pp. 712-6.
Gilman, R. (1991) 'The Eco-Village Challenge', in In Context, # 29, pp. 10-14. (Also available at http://www.context.org/ICLIB/IC29/Gilman2.htm)
Gilman, R., & Gilman, D. (1991) Eco-villages and Sustainable Communities. Bainbridge Island, USA: Context Institute.
Greenberg, D. (1993) Growing Up in Community: Children and Education Within Contemporary Intentional Communities. Unpublished PhD Thesis, University of Minnesota, USA. (to arrange access to this, email: daniel@ic.org)
Hall, J. (2000) Apocalypse Observed. London: Routledge.
Hanson, C. (1996) The Cohousing Handbook. Vancouver: Hartley & Marks.
Hardy, D. (1979) Alternative Communities in Nineteenth Century England. London, UK: Longmans.
Hardy, D. (2000) Utopian England: Community Experiments 1900-1945. London, UK: E. & F.N. Spon.
Hockerton Housing Members (2001) The Sustainable Community: A Practical Guide. Southwell, UK: Hockerton Housing Project.
Hofer, S. (1998) The Hutterites: Lives and Images of a Communal People. Saskatoon, Canada: Hofer Publications.
Hostetler, J. & Huntington G. (1996) The Hutterites in North America. Fort Worth, USA: Harcourt Brace & Co.
Introvigne, M. (1996) 'Damanhur: A Magical community in Italy', in Communal Societies, vol 16, pp. 71-84.
Introvigne, M. (2003) 'Damanhur', in K. Christensen and D. Levinson, (eds), Encyclopedia of Community: From the Village to the Virtual World. Thousand Oaks, USA: Sage, pp. 111-2.
Jackson, H. & Svensson, K. (2002) Ecovillage Living: Restoring the Earth and Her People. Totnes, UK: Gaia Trust/Green Books.
Janzen, D. et al (1996) Fire, Salt and Peace: Intentional Christian Communities Alive in North America. Evanston, USA: Shalom Mission Communities.
Kanter R. (1972) Commitment and Community: Communes and Utopias in Social Perspective. Cambridge: Harvard University Press.
Kennedy, M. & Kennedy, D. (1997) Designing Ecological Settlements. Berlin, Germany: Dieter Reimer Verlag and European Academy of the Urban Environment.
Kinkade, K. (1994) Is It Utopia Yet? An Insider's View of Twin Oaks Community in its 26th Year. Louisa, USA: Twin Oaks Community.
Klee-Hartzell, M. (1996) 'The Oneida Community Family', in Communal Societies, # 16, pp. 15-22.
Kozeny, G. (2000) 'Red Carpets and Slammed Doors: Visiting Communities', in Communities

Directory: A Guide to Intentional Communities and Cooperative Living. Rutledge, USA: Fellowship for Intentional Communities, pp. 35-40.
Kraybill, D. & Bowman, C. (2001) On the Backroad to Heaven. Baltimore: John Hopkins University Press.
Manuel, F. & Manuel, F. (1979) Utopian Thought in the Western World. Cambridge, USA: Harvard University Press.
Matarese, S. & Salmon, P. (1995) Assessing Psychopathology in Communal Societies', in Communal Societies, vol. 15, pp. 25-54.
McCamant, K. & Durrett, G. (1994) Cohousing: A Contemporary Approach to Housing Ourselves. Berkeley: Habitat Press.
McDougall, B. (2003) 'Going Green in the Burbs', in Canadian Geographic, Jan/Feb, pp. 66-74.
McKanan, D. (2003) 'Intentional Individuals: Growing Up in Radical Christian Communities', in Communal Societies, vol. 23, pp. 129-44.
McLaughlin C. & Davidson, G. (1985) Builders of the Dawn. Shutesbury, USA: Sirius.
Melton, G. (2003) 'Cults', in K. Christensen and D. Levinson, (eds), Encyclopedia of Community: From the Village to the Virtual World. Thousand Oaks, USA: Sage, pp. 357-60.
Meltzer, G. (1999) 'Cohousing: Linking Community and Sustainability', in Communal Societies vol. # 19, pp. 85-100.
Meltzer, G. (forthcoming) Cohousing: Integrating Social and Environmental Sustainability.
Merrifield, J. (1998) Damanhur: The Real Dream. Hammersmith, UK: Thorsons/Harper Collins.
Metcalf, W. (1993) 'Findhorn: Routinization of Charisma', in Communal Societies, vol. 13, pp. 1-21.
Metcalf, W. (1995) From Utopian Dreaming to Communal Reality: Cooperative Lifestyles in Australia. Sydney, Australia: University of New South Wales Press.
Metcalf, W. (1996) Shared Visions, Shared Lives: Communal Living Around the Globe. Forres, UK: Findhorn Press.
Metcalf, W. (1998) The Gayndah Communes. Rockhampton, Australia: Central Queensland University Press.
Metcalf, W. & Huf, E. (2002) Herrnhut: Australia's First Utopian Commune. Melbourne, Australia: Melbourne University Press.
Metcalf, W. (2003) 'Intentional Communities in Australia and New Zealand', in K. Christensen and D. Levinson, (eds), Encyclopedia of Community: From the Village to the Virtual World. Thousand Oaks, USA: Sage, pp. 705-12.
Metcalf, W. (2003) 'Intentional Communities in Latin America', in K. Christensen and D. Levinson, (eds), Encyclopedia of Community: From the Village to the Virtual World. Thousand Oaks, USA: Sage, pp. 744-7.
Metcalf, W. (2003) 'ZEGG', in K. Christensen and D. Levinson, (eds), Encyclopedia of Community: From the Village to the Virtual World. Thousand Oaks, USA: Sage, pp. 1493-4.
Miller, T. (1991) The Hippies and American Values. Knoxville, USA: University of Tennessee Press.
Miller, T. (1998) The Quest for Utopia in Twentieth-Century America. Syracuse, USA: Syracuse University Press.
Miller, T. (1999) The 60s Communes. Syracuse, USA: Syracuse University Press.
Mohanty, B. (2003) 'Intentional Communities in India', in K. Christensen and D. Levinson, (eds), The Encyclopedia of Community: From the Village to the Virtual World. Thousand Oaks,

USA: Sage, pp. 723-7.
Near, H. (1992 & 1997)The Kibbutz Movement: A History. Volumes I & 2, London, UK & Oregon, USA: Littman Library and Oxford University Press.
Near, H. (2003) 'Intentional Communities in Israel—History', in K. Christensen and D. Levinson, (eds), Encyclopedia of Community: From the Village to the Virtual World. Thousand Oaks, USA: Sage, pp. 731-6.
Oved, Y. (1986) Two Hundred Years of American Communes. New Brunswick, USA: Transaction Books.
Oved, Y. (1996) The Witness of the Brothers. New Brunswick, USA: Transaction Publications.
Oved, Y. (2000) 'Communal Movements in the Twentieth Century', in R. Schaer, G. Clayes and L. Sargent (eds) Utopia-The Search for the Ideal Society in the Western World. New York: Oxford University Press, pp. 268-78.
Pitzer, D. (1989) 'Developmental Communalism: An Alternative Approach to Communal Studies', in D. Hardy and L. Davidson, (eds), Utopian Thought and Communal Experience. Enfield, UK: Middlesex Polytechnic, pp. 68-76; also in Diggers & Dreamers 92/93, Winslow, UK: Communities Network, pp. 85-92.
Pitzer, D. (1997) America's Communal Utopias, Chapel Hill, USA: University of North Carolina Press.
Pitzer, D. (2003) 'Intentional Communities in the United States and Canada—History', in K. Christensen and D. Levinson, (eds), Encyclopedia of Community: From the Village to the Virtual World. Thousand Oaks, USA: Sage, pp. 762-71.
Pochat, J. 'Intentional Communities in France', in K. Christensen and D. Levinson, (eds), Encyclopedia of Community: From the Village to the Virtual World. Thousand Oaks, USA: Sage, pp. 716-8.
Poldervaart, S., Jansen, H. & Kesler, B. (eds) (2001) Contemporary Utopian Struggles. Amsterdam: Aksant.
Pope, P. (1992) Neither Angels Nor Demons. London, UK: Century Random House.
Tower, L. (2000) 'Utopia and the Late Twentieth Century', in R. Schaer, G. Clayes and L. Sargent, (eds), Utopia-The Search for the Ideal Society in the Western World. New York: Oxford University Press, pp. 333-46.
Scott, A. (1997) The Promise of Paradise. Vancouver, Canada: Whitecap.
Schaub, L. (2003) 'Intentional Communities in the United States and Canada—Current', in K. Christensen and D. Levinson, (eds), Encyclopedia of Community: From the Village to the Virtual World. Thousand Oaks, USA: Sage, pp. 758-62.
Smith, W. (2001) 'Families in Contemporary Intentional Communities: Diversity and Purpose', in Communal Societies, vol. 21, pp. 79-93.
Stockwell, F. (1998) Encyclopedia of American Communes. Jefferson, USA: McFarland & Co.
Sullivan, B. (1994) The Dawning of Auroville. Auroville, India: Auroville Press.
Sullivan, B. (2003) 'Auroville', in K. Christensen and D. Levinson, (eds), Encyclopedia of Community: From the Village to the Virtual World. Thousand Oaks, USA: Sage, pp. 74-6.
Schwartz, W. and Schwartz, D. (1998) Living Lightly: Travels in Post-Consumer Society. Charlbury (UK): Jon Carpenter Publishing.
Talbott, J. (1993) Simply Build Green. Findhorn (UK): Findhorn Press.
Van der Ryn, S. and Calthorpe, P. (1991) Sustainable Communities. San Francisco (USA): Sierra Club Books.
Wagner, J. (1985) 'Success in Intentional Communities: The Problem of Evaluation', in Communal Societies, vol. 5, pp 89-100.

Wagner, J. (1986) 'Sexuality and Gender Roles in Utopian Communities: A Critical Survey of Scholarly Work', in Communal Societies, vol. 6, pp. 172-88.
Weisbrod, C. (1992) 'Communal Groups and the Larger Society: Legal Dilemmas', in Communal Societies, vol. 12, pp. 1-19.
Zablocki, B. (1980) Alienation and Charisma: A study of Contemporary American Communes. New York (USA): Free Press.

Directories

Communities Directory: A Guide to Intentional Communities and Cooperative Living. (2000), Rutledge, USA: Fellowship for Intentional Communities. Covers North American intentional communities with some international coverage.
(http://fic.ic.org)
Diggers & Dreamers: The Guide to Communal Living. (2003), London, UK: D&D Publications. (Compiled by S. Bunker, et al). Covers intentional communities in Great Britain and Ireland with some international coverage.
(http://www.diggersanddreamers.org.uk)
Directory of Communal Living in Aotearoa. (forthcoming), Christchurch, New Zealand: STRAW Umbrella Trust. Will describe and provide contacts for a wide range of intentional communities in New Zealand.
(email: straw@paradise.net.nz)
Directory of Ecovillages in Europe. (1999), Ginsterweg, Germany: Global Ecovillage Network. (Compiled by B. Grindheim and D. Kennedy), Global Eco-village network. Excellent coverage of European ecovillages but not other types of intentional communities.
(email: info@gen-europe.org)
Eco-Villages & Communities in Australia and New Zealand. (2000) Maleny, Australia: Global Ecovillage Network. (Compiled by B. Knudson). (http://genoa.ecovillage.org/genoceania/products/index.html)
Ecovillage Travels in Europe. (2002), offers a booking service and advice on how to visit and stay at numerous European ecovillages ranging from Suomineito Yhteiso in Finland and Sólheimer in Iceland, to Kibbutz Lotan in Israel and Ekofoca in Turkey. (compiled by L. Borio and S. Reichmuth)
(email: info@gen-europe.org)
Encyclopedia of Large Intentional Communities. (2003) Compiled and regularly updated by R. Gering. This compilation is the project of a very dedicated German academic, and contains information not easily available elsewhere.
(http://groups.yahoo.com/group/INTENTIONALCOMMUNITIES/files/DIRECTORIES)
Eurotopia: Directory of Intentional Communities and Ecovillages in Europe. (2000) Poppau, Germany: Silke Hagmaier Verlag. (Compiled by S. Hagmaier, et al). A wide ranging directory of all sorts of intentional communities throughout Europe. A new edition of Eurotopia is expected in April, 2004
(http://www.eurotopia.de)
From Here to Nirvana: The Yoga Journal Guide to Spiritual India. (1998) New York, USA: Riverhead Books (by A. Cushman and J. Jones). Coverage of spiritually based intentional communities in India.
(http://www.amazon.co.uk)
Global Ecovillage Network Information Service. This web-based directory lists ecovillages, associ-

ated events and other relevant information.
(http://gen.ecovillage.org/iservices/)
Global Ecovillage Network Living and Learning Centres. A small brochure helping people who wish to visit European ecovillages. Compiled by Marti Mueller.
(email: info@gen-europe.org)
Rural Landsharing Community Association. This provides a directory to a wide range of intentional communities in northern New South Wales, Australia.
(http://www.jindibah-community.org/rlca)
Spiritual Britain: A Practical Guide to Today's Spiritual Communities, Centres and Sacred Places (1998) Hong Kong: Pilgrims' Travel Guides (Compiled by P. Lloyd).
(http://www.amazon.co.uk or email: pilgrim@iohk.com)

International Scholarly Research Groups

International Communal Studies Association, with headquarters in Israel, includes people from intentional communities and those interested in studying historical and contemporary communal groups around the globe.
(http://www.ic.org/icsa)
The ICSA conference, held at ZEGG, Germany, in 2001, was called Communal Living on the Threshold of a New Millenium: Lessons and Perspectives. The proceedings are available at: http://www.ic.org/icsa/conference.html
Communal Studies Association, with headquarters in USA, includes people interested in studying historical and contemporary intentional communities, as well as some intentional community members. They publish the scholarly journal, Communal Societies.
(http://www.communalstudies.org)
Society for Utopian Studies, mainly in USA and Canada, consists of scholars and lay people who are interested in utopianism in literature and psychology, as well as how utopianism is implemented within intentional communities. They publish the scholarly journal, Utopian Studies.
(http://www.utoronto.ca/utopia)
Utopian Studies Society Europe, mainly in Europe, comprised of people who are interested in European utopian literature and intentional communities.
(http://www.utopianstudieseurope.org)

Scholarly Intentional Community Research Centres

Center for Communal Studies
Director: Dr Don Pitzer
At University of Southern Indiana, Evansville, USA.
web site: http://www.communalcenter.org
email: dpitzer@usi.edu
Department of Communal Research
Director: Professor Yaacov Oved
At Yad Tabenkin Research and Documentation Center of the Kibbutz Movement, Ramat Efal, Israel.
no web site
email: ruthsy-t@bezeqint.net

Academic, Scholarly Journals

Communal Societies contains scholarly research articles about intentional communities around the globe. It is published annually by the Communal Studies Association.
(http://www.communalstudies.org/journals/csvol1.shtml)
Utopian Studies contains scholarly research articles about utopianism and utopian endeavours, including intentional communities. It is published annually by the Society for Utopian Studies.
(http://www.utoronto.ca/utopia/journal)

Major Magazines and Newsletters

Chip 'N' Away newsletter. Covers intentional communities in New Zealand.
(email: dave.chipnaway@inet.net.nz)
Cohousing. This is produced by the Cohousing Association of United States, and reports on cohousing communities from around the world.
(http://www.cohousing.org/services/journal)
Communes at Large Letter. Published in Israel by kibbutzniks, with witty and insightful international coverage of all forms of intentional communities.
(http://www.communa.org.il)
Communities. Published by the Fellowship for Intentional Community (USA), with great coverage of intentional community matters, some of which is international. (http://www.ic.org/cmag)
Global Ecovillage Network News Service. Contains articles about the broad range of ecovillages, and ecovillage networking around the world.
(http://gen.ecovillage.org/iservices/)
Permaculture Activist. Mainly about permaculture, but occasionally has articles about intentional communities.
(http://www.permacultureactivist.net)
Permaculture Magazine. Mainly UK coverage but with increasing international scope. Has some coverage of intentional communities, and has a regular section discussing ecovillage issues.
(http://www.permaculture.co.uk/mag/home.html)

Videos & CD Roms

Crystal Waters Permaculture Village. (1999) Producer: Global Ecovillage Network. Fourteen minutes, describes Crystal Waters, a large intentional community in Australia, and identifies the key tenets of ecovillage design.
Available as CD Rom or video (NTSC or PAL format).
(http://genoa.ecovillage.org/genoceania/products/index.html)
Damanhur: A Great Adventure. (2003) Producer: SynerGea. Covers the story of Damanhur, Italy, with fantastic pictures of their underground chambers, The Temple of Mankind.
(http://www.synergea.it)
Ecovillages in Europe. (2002) Producers: Agnieszka Komoch and Eduard Gonzalez. A CD Rom which looks at many European ecovillages including Findhorn Foundation and Torri Superiore, and provides information about ecovillage design, economy, conflict resolution, education, etc.
(http://www.gen-europe.org/e-shop)
Ecovillages: The Dream and the Dreamers. (2001) Producer: Michael Tarkowski. Documentary of an ecovillage meeting in Poland.

(http://www.gen-europe.org/e-shop)
The Findhorn Foundation: Straight From the Heart. (1995) Producer: Sam O'Brien. Covers daily life as well as the spiritual basis for this intentional community in Scotland.
(http://www.findhorn.org/store)
Follow the Dirt Road: An Introduction to Intentional Communities in the 1990s. (1991) Producer: Monique Gauthier. Examines life within a wide range of intentional communities including The Farm, Twin Oaks, Ananda, Celo and Shannon Farm.
(email: monique@ic.org)
The Future of Paradise. (2000) Producer: Michael Murray. This video is based on the tour of ten successful European ecovillages by David Kanaley, the Planning Director of Byron Bay Shire Council, Australia. It examines, from a town planner's perspective, what works/fails, practically and socially.
(email: michael@byronpropertysearch.com.au)
Habitat Revolution. (1998) Producer: Global Village Video. Offers an overview, plus many insights into ecovillages such as The Farm, Crystal Waters and Findhorn Foundation, in several countries, and addresses intentional community issues such as spirituality, sustainability and decision-making.
(http://www.farmcatalog.com/community.htm)
Visions of Utopia: Experiments in Sustainable Culture. (2002) Producer: Geoph Kozeny. During 94 minutes, this profiles seven intentional communities: Camphill Special School, Twin Oaks, Breitenbush Hot Springs, Purple Rose Collective, Earthaven Ecovillage, Ananda Village, and Nyland Cohousing.
(http://fic.ic.org/video)
ZEGG: A Presentation of a Cultural Model. (1997) Producers: Heidi Snel and Malcolm St Julian-Brown. A superb insight into ZEGG, Germany, one of the most interesting intentional communities in the world today.
(email: ramona.stucki@t-online.de)

Tertiary Education Within Intentional Communities

Ecological Solutions. Based at Crystal Waters, a large Australian ecovillage, they offer a range of tertiary level courses which are accredited by institutions such as Pacific Lutheran College (USA), Chuo University (Japan), and Stellenbosch University (South Africa).
(http://www.ecologicalsolutions.com.au)
Findhorn Foundation College. Offers tertiary level courses in a range of subjects, some directly relevant to intentional community, within the experiential context of life in the Findhorn Foundation community. Most courses are accredited by Findhorn Foundation College. The Findhorn Community Semester is a study abroad program accredited at bachelors level by Pacific Lutheran University, USA.
(http://www.findhorncollege.org)
Living Routes - Ecovillage Education. Offers residential educational experiences and accredited tertiary courses at intentional communities in Europe, India, Australia, Senegal, Brazil and the USA.
(http://www.livingroutes.org)

Organisations of and for Intentional Community

Cohousing Association of the United States. Lists cohousing groups, details resources, informa-

tion, classified ads, cohousing news, etc. They also publish the bimonthly Cohousing Journal.
(http://www.cohousing.org)
Federation of Egalitarian Communities (FEC) is a network of income-sharing communal groups in North America.
(http://www.thefec.org)
Fellowship for Intentional Community (FIC). Members come mostly from North American intentional communities. FIC publishes the magazine, Communities, and Communities Directory.
(http://fic.ic.org)
FIC also has a mail order service for books and videos about intentional community.
(http://store.ic.org)
Global Ecovillage Network (GEN) has offices throughout the world, to represent and promote the interests of ecovillages on all continents.
General Gen contact: http://gen.ecovillage.org
Ecovillage Network of the Americas: http://ena.ecovillage.org
GEN Europe/Africa: http://www.gen-europe.org
GEN Oceania/Asia, including Australia and New Zealand: http://genoa.ecovillage.org

Websites

There are numerous internet sites where people can discuss all aspects of intentional community life. Some of those known to me are:
Intentionalcommunities: http://groups.yahoo.com/group/intentionalcommunities/join
Intentional Communities: http://groups.yahoo.com/group/intentional-communities/join
Global Ecovillage Network: http://www.ecovillage.org/ecobalance
For scholars and members of intentional communities: http://www2.h-net.msu.edu/lists/subscribe.cgi
For scholarly discussion of utopias and utopianism: http://www2.h-net.msu.edu/~utopia/
Australian National Intentional Communities Association: http://groups.yahoo.com/subscribe/anica
Many websites offer general information about intentional communities. Some of these, with web site or email address, are:
Asociación Gaia - Argentina Communities Network: http://www.gaia.org.ar
Austrian National Ecovillage Network. email: martin.kirchner@gmx.net
Bangladesh Ecovillage Network. email: mccoy@bdonline.com
Bolivian Ecovillage Network: http://groups.msn.com/ilppictures
Brazilian Ecovillage Network: http://ena.ecovillage.org/English/news/2002/wsf-br-report.html
Centre for Alternative Technology, UK: http://www.cat.org.uk
CoHousing Company, USA: http://www.cohousingco.com
CoHousing Association of the United States: http://www.cohousing.org
Czech Republic Ecovillage Network: http://www.permalot.cz
Danish Association of Sustainable Communities - LOS: http://europe.ecovillage.org/denmark/network
Dutch Ecovillage Network. email: kyrakuitert@hotmail.com
Ecovillage Network of Canada: http://ena.ecovillage.org/enc
Ecovillage Network of the Americas: http://ena.ecovillage.org
Ecovillage Resource Links: http://www.eco-village.cjb.net

Ecovillages Around the World: http://gen.ecovillage.org
European intentional communities: http://www.eurotopia.de
Finnish Ecovillage Network. email: kataja.maki@sci.fi
Forming and facilitating intentional community: http://www.creating-a-life-together.org
French Ecovillage Network (Reseau Francais des Ecovillages). email: jeanmi3@hotmail.com
Gaia Trust, Denmark: http://www.gaia.org
GEN Europe: http://www.gen-europe.org
GEN Oceania and Asia: http://genoa.ecovillage.org
German Communities Network (Come Together Netzwerk). email: flein@gmx.de or d.federlein@gmx.de
Global Ecovillage Network Information Service: (http://gen.ecovillage.org/iservices)
Hungary, Ecovillage Gyürüfü. email: gyurufu@mail.matav.hu or tarkaret@freemail.hu
Intentional communities in UK: http://www.utopia-britannica.org.uk
IPEC - Permaculture and Ecovillages Institute of Cerrado, Brazil: http://www.permacultura.org.br/ipec
Israel National Ecovillage Contact. email: ml-lotan@zahav.net.il
Italian Ecovillage Network (Rete Italiana dei Villagi Ecologici). email: aam-red@greenplanet.net
Locating Intentional Communities: http://www.ic.org
Mexican Ecovillages - Red de Ecoaldeas de México: http://www.laneta.apc.org/rem
New Zealand Ecovillage and Cohousing Network: http://www.converge.org.nz/evcnz
Nippon Ecovillage Network, Japan: http://www.ap-world.com/nenproject
Norwegian Ecovillage Network (Alternativt Nettverk). email: osolum@online.no
Permaculture Centre of Japan. email: bzb03643@nifty.ne.jp
Polish Ecovillage Network - WAS. email: wasnicole@wp.pl
Portuguese Ecovillage Network. email: comunidade.verde@mail.pt or pedro.macedo@mail.pt
Romanian National Ecovillage Contact. email: visator@home.ro
Russian Ecovillage Network. email: vasudeva@mail.spb.org
Spanish Ecovillages - Red Ibérica de Ecoaldeas: http://selba.solidaragon.org
Sri Lankan Ecovillages - Sarvodaya Dhamsak: http://www.sarvodaya.org
Swedish National Association for Ecological Living (Ekoboforeningen Njord). email: njord@telia.com or gunlaug@arch.kth.se
Turkish Ecovillage Network - Ekilat. email: idemet@metu.edu.tr
UK Ecovillage Network: http://europe.ecovillage.org/uk/network
Urban Ecology, Australia: http://www.urbanecology.org.au
Urban Ecology Center, USA: http://my.execpc.com~uec/
U.S. East Ecovillage Network: http://ena.ecovillage.org/english/region/USEast/index.html
U.S. West Ecovillage Network: http://ena.ecovillage.org/english/region/USWest/index.html

---

1. Earlier versions of my research for parts of chapter 3 have appeared in: *Diggers and Dreamers* 2000 / 2001, (eds) S. Bunker et al.., London: D&D Publications, 1999; *Creating Harmony: Conflict Resolution in Community,* (ed) Hildur Jackson, Storkevaenger, Denmark: Gaia Trust, & East Meon, UK: Permaculture Publications, 1999; *Eurotopia: Directory of Intentional Communities and Ecovillages in Europe,* (eds) S. Hagmaier et al, Poppau, Germany: Ökodorf Sieben Linden, 2000; and *Encyclopedia of Community: From the Village to the Virtual World,* (eds) K. Christensen & D. Levinson, Thousand Oaks, USA: Sage, 2003.